Succeeding at Your Interview

A Practical Guide for Teachers

SUCCEEDING AT YOUR INTERVIEW

A PRACTICAL GUIDE FOR TEACHERS

Rita S. Brause
Fordham University

Christine P. Donohue
Fordham University

Alice W. Ryan
St. Joseph's College

LEA LAWRENCE ERLBAUM ASSOCIATES, PUBLISHERS
2002 Mahwah, New Jersey London

Lawrence Erlbaum Associates, Inc., Publishers
10 Industrial Avenue
Mahwah, New Jersey 07430

Cover design by Kathryn Houghtaling Lacey

Library of Congress Cataloging-in-Publication Data

Brause, Rita S.
Succeeding at your interview : a practical guide for teachers / Rita S. Brause, Christine P. Donohue, Alice W. Ryan.
p. cm.
Includes bibliographical references and index.
ISBN 0-8058-3856-2 (pbk. : alk. paper)
1. Teachers—Employment—United States—Handbooks, manuals, etc.
2. Teaching—Vocational guidance—United States—Handbooks, manuals, etc.
3. Employment interviewing—Handbooks, manuals, etc. 4. Job hunting—Handbooks, manuals, etc. I. Title: Succeeding at your interview. II. Donohue, Christine P. III. Ryan, Alice W. IV. Title
LB1780.B69 2001
650.14 024 372—dc21 2001-033002
CIP

Books published by Lawrence Erlbaum Associates are printed on acid-free paper, and their bindings are chosen for strength and durability.

Printed in the United States of America
10 9 8 7 6 5 4

Contents

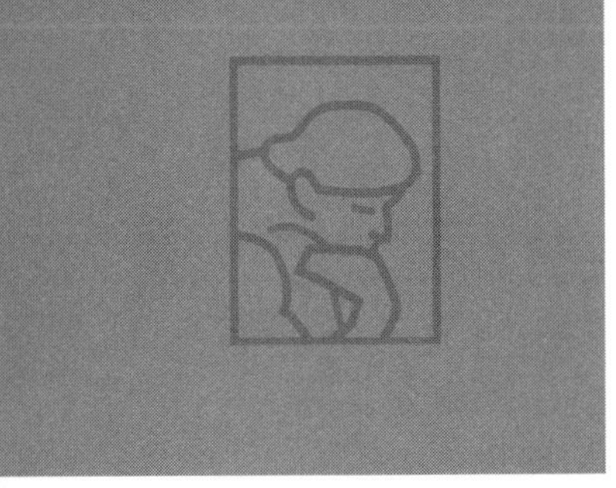

PREFACE

When you decided to become a teacher, you took the first step on your professional journey. While re-creating yourself as a teacher, you are gathering information about teaching practices and school environments. You want to teach in a school that is a good match to your beliefs and style. You want to find a good match between your strengths and a specific school's needs. How can you find the right place to start your teaching career? The possibilities are numerous. *Succeeding at Your Interview* addresses these questions.

As a candidate, you have choices to consider and decisions to make. We ease your task by presenting comprehensive information that will help you engage in a broad range of activities and build your confidence on the road to success.

There are literally thousands of teaching openings, but each setting is unique. Each school system establishes its own rules developed over many years. One school may provide an extensive mentorship program. Another may encourage autonomy and self-reliance. Some schools offer an interdisciplinary curriculum, whereas others concentrate on highly specialized courses of study. You'll want to find a setting that matches your geographic boundaries and educational concerns, respects your unique qualities, and makes you feel welcome. As you think in terms of self-promotion, identify the special talents, experiences, and qualities you will bring to your classroom. Set your qualifications apart from others who are competing for the same position.

WHAT CAN YOU EXPECT ON YOUR INTERVIEW JOURNEY?

Many of the interview highlights shown in Fig. P.1 are typical, some predictable, and some optional. Although each of us searches for teaching positions through different journeys, there are signposts to recognize. Your path may include a brief screening, a writing sample, an in-depth interview, and a demonstration lesson. Or you may be asked to respond to an automated phone screening. Alternatively, bypassing the main road totally, a district may rely on personal recommendations or select a teacher from the list of substitute teachers serving the school.

These different pathways provide some glimpses into the school's priorities that may influence your decision. When you read about

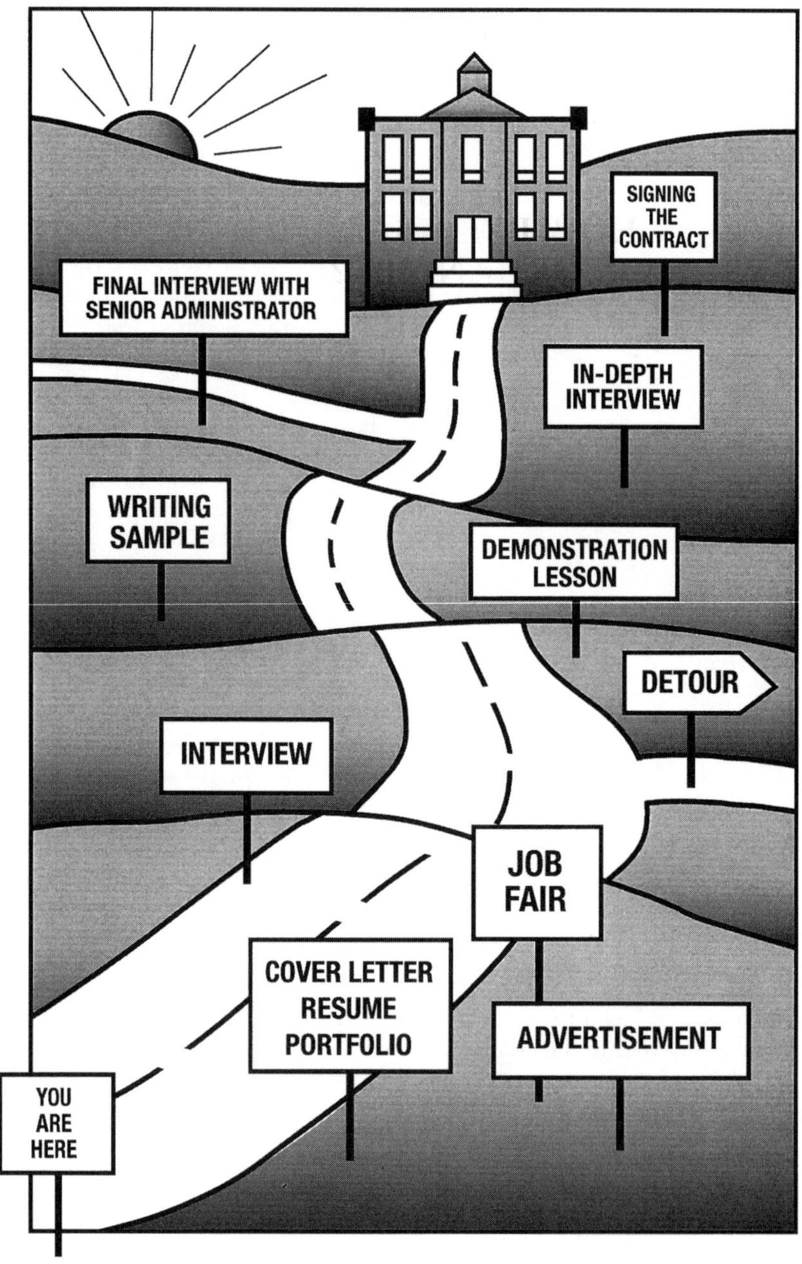

FIG. P.1. An interview journey.

each milestone, you will begin to understand the varied routes taken in the search. You and the school or district have many options along the way. [We use the terms school and district interchangeably.]

We systematically collected a wealth of information from experienced school administrators, faculty, and parents at all educational levels. After analyzing many hours of taped interviews, conversations, focus group sessions, and published documents, we are able to offer multiple perspectives on interviewing.

HOW IS THIS BOOK ORGANIZED?

Although books are typically organized for sequential reading (e.g., read page 1 before page 21), *Succeeding at Your Interview: A Practical Guide for Teachers* emulates an Internet environment within a print context. This book is uniquely structured, drawing on evolving technologies and grounding your reading with a problem-based focus. You will view multiple distinct windows or dialog boxes. The problem-based focus assists you in reaching your specific, clearly defined goal—finding a teaching position. Ultimately, we help you design a successful job search. The process is organized into five major parts, each of which is highlighted by the gray thumb tabs at the book's edge. These carefully spaced tabs ease your access to each of the separate parts.

The five parts of the book guide us through the interview journey. Each part is comprised of two or three chapters and a scenario. The chapters concentrate on a particular aspect of the process you need to address, and the scenario simulates typical interview experiences. Each chapter starts with a combination of a brief verbal overview and a graphic organizer (called At a Glance) identifying the major issues addressed in the chapter and ends with a Summing Up section presenting text accompanied by an expanded graphic organizer, noting the details discussed extensively within the chapter.

Part A: Starting Your Search

As we read the first interview scenario, we see how Steve's resourcefulness resulted in his getting an interview for a position, as well as the pacing and content of an initial interview. Chapters 1 and 2 then address basic issues on accessing information and focusing your options through careful decision making.

Part B: Getting Ready to Apply

Reading Jennifer's interview with a school-based team, we see how a candidate was able to use her careful preparation to provide consequential, significant information to the interview committee. Chapters 3 and 4 suggest ways to organize efficient systems to create and assemble effective résumés and other essential materials.

Part C: Knowing the Process

We meet Felicia, whose second interview involves a role play, one of many activities you may encounter as you interview. Chapters 5 and 6 introduce a broad range of screening activities and guide your practice responses.

Part D: Preparing Yourself

Marcy's interview with several principals (a second-level interview) provides insight into the types of questions you might experience when meeting with educators who have different perspectives on professional practice. Chapters 7, 8, and 9 provide guided practice in responding to interview questions, reflecting on typical responses, and communicating your confidence (even when you wish you were more confident).

Part E: Reflecting on Your Journey

Kippi's interview and demonstration lesson provide another sample of the interview experience. Chapters 10 and 11 offer ideas to reflect on and learn from your interview and ways to continue your journey.

The scenarios spaced throughout the book simulate typical interview situations with Steve, Jennifer, Felicia, Marcy, and Kippi. They reflect frequent occurrences in a wide range of interview formats and purposes (initial interviews and second interviews, one-to-one interviews, and interviews with many participants).

These are not models, they are not verbatim transcripts, and they are not to be memorized for use during your interview. Rather, as you "eavesdrop" on the interviews, you will be looking at specific interactions and contemplating some useful generalizations to remember in your job search. You will understand how each candidate arrived at the interview, a major feat in itself! And you will consider multiple strategies for responding at interviews.

As these scenarios evolve, they increase your sensitivity to the pacing, the interactions, and the information exchanges that you, too, are likely to experience at interviews. The scenario format will help you understand the strategies others have used in seeking information about openings, obtaining interviews, and negotiating interactions.

Margin notes posed strategically through the text encourage your engagement, asking you to interpret remarks and speculate about important issues. In an escalating process, you will respond to questions designed to promote your analysis.

Keep in Mind comments enhance your contemplation of our interpretations as these interviews unfold. (You will be directed to these remarks with numerical superscripts that refer to the window on the lower half of the page; e.g., [1].)

Your Response boxes guide your analysis of issues and help you create special notes. In some chapters you are given explicit direction; later, we scaffold the development of your personal response: reviewing your response, reflecting on it, and developing it more fully. This multistep activity leads to a greater awareness of essential characteristics of strong, winning responses.

Search/Find boxes facilitate your accumulation of a wide range of information that will be important in creating your application packet and pursuing positions. By jotting down details requested in numerous documents, for example, you will expedite your preparation of essential materials.

Through these multiple windows you may critique and clarify your thinking as you draft and revise your responses. The scenarios provide a holistic view of the interview process. In addition to mining the subtleties inherent in interviews, we explicitly document the knowledge essential to succeed.

WHAT IS YOUR ROLE AS A READER?

Having the opportunity to choose from a series of linked windows, you will select the window(s) that will enhance your journey at each particular junction. You may choose to explore an issue in depth or bypass it until a later time when it might be more meaningful for you. You may find it more productive to read all of the scenarios first, or all of the numbered chapters, or you may find it most effective to read the book in the sequence in which it is presented. Some will benefit from reading the scenarios exclusively, returning for a second reading to contemplate the Keep in Mind comments, which highlight subtle, potentially bypassed issues. Others may prefer the opportunity to reflect on

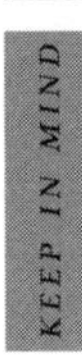

[1]This is the place where you will find our Keep in Mind comments.

the experience with the assistance of the margin notes on the first go-round. (When you need more space to note your ideas, use the blank pages throughout the book.) As you read the text, we encourage your constant reflection and response.

Three factors contribute to your success in becoming a teacher: the knowledge you have developed during your teacher education program, your ability to communicate that knowledge and experience, and your confidence. *Succeeding at Your Interview: A Practical Guide for Teachers,* no doubt, will enhance your ability to project your professionalism. Coupled with your resilient, adventuresome spirit, you will be on the path to success. Let's get on with your journey!

ACKNOWLEDGMENTS

Researching and writing *Succeeding at Your Interview* over the past 4 years has been a memorable journey for us individually and collectively. We have learned to write in new and exciting ways while examining the increasingly complex world of teaching and interviewing.

Our book has benefitted from the generous cooperation of many educators who freely gave of their time and their expertise in the interest of helping neophytes enter the wonderful world of teaching. Some of our colleagues met in focus groups, some shared stories informally, and some provided documents. We are indebted to all, including Lori Aidala, Barbara Borriati, Eric Byrne, Toby Cohen, Jane Dorian, Betsy Einenger, Donna Franquinha, Evelyn Fulton, Carolyn Gear, Doug Goffman, Gary Goldstein, Gail Gottlieb, Jill Harrington, Jill Hayden, Irene Hyman, Selma Katz, Rosanne Lerner Kurstedt, Barbara Lapetina, Hindy List, Bernadette McBride, Jennifer Penha, Marylou Ragno, Mary Roberts, Jennifer Satriale, Rita Seidenberg, and Diane Trupia.

Most of the time, as we deliberated over each word of our drafts, we were happily ensconced in the St. John's University Law School lounge, where Andrew J. McLaughlin graciously welcomed us.

Naomi Silverman, Senior Editor at Lawrence Erlbaum Associates, Inc., our guiding light and constant supporter, along with Lori Hawver, her dedicated assistant, were always at the ready, guiding us in important ways and providing enthusiastic encouragement. Linda Eisenberg, Senior Production Editor, provided insightful, generous comments. The LEA team has exemplified an ideal academic community for us. Stephen M. Koziol of Michigan State University and Maia Pank Mertz of Ohio State University offered valuable comments and suggestions that improved the book considerably.

Mitchell Strear, our Fordham colleague, not only sought the responses of the Fordham teaching interns to some of our questions, but also encouraged us to "finish the book!" so his students could benefit from it.

Marcy Donohue provided us with excellent technical support, particularly at times when we were frustrated with our technical ineptness. Jeff Haney of MJGraphixs expertly translated our formatting ideas into professional, creative representations that clarified our text. Timothy W. Gerken enthusiastically transformed some of our graphic scribbles into clear drawings.

Irene Eddy brought her efficiency and knowledge of format to her thoughtful comments, helping us to move our project along. Jackie Kazarian generously provided our end piece drawing depicting a joyful candidate victorious after the journey. Christine Cunningham and Cynthia Barrett also provided very valuable professional support as we navigated the development of our manuscript.

We appreciate the faculty grants provided by St. Joseph's College and the Fordham University Office of Research toward the development of this book.

We had wonderful reviewers whose recommendations helped us to reach this point, namely Roberta C. Brause, Joseph E. Donohue, and Mary Theresa Downs.

We are grateful to these wonderful people, all of whom are exemplary educators in the truest sense of the word. We are blessed with their friendship.

Although there are many who helped us get to this point, to whom we are indebted, we dedicate this book to three remarkable people who supported our work in very special ways:

Roberta C. Brause   Joseph E. Donohue   Maurice J. Ryan

We recognize the extraordinary camaraderie and collegiality of our writing team, each of whom contributed equally and uniquely in these endeavors. We will miss the sharing of ideas and the daily struggles to find the right words. We suspect that there is another book waiting in the wings and put all on notice . . . be prepared for the next venture!

LIST OF TABLES

LIST OF FIGURES

PART A

STARTING YOUR SEARCH

The first step in starting your search is gathering information that is essential in deciding where to apply. Part A provides information in two contexts—Steve's Scenario and Chapters 1 and 2. As you eavesdrop on Steve's interview you will understand some of his job search techniques. Taking the "fly on the wall" view in the principal's office, you will get a sense of the content and rhythm of Steve's interview, a representative sample of many such interactions.

You might ask, "Where in the world do I begin?" Chapter 1 will broaden your understanding of the formal and informal ways to obtain information about schools and help you to pinpoint the places where you are likely to find job openings.

After searching advertisements and visiting job sites and Web sites, you are ready to consider your many options. Will you relocate? Do you want to work with young children or are older students more aligned with your preparation? Will you seek a position as a specialist or a generalist? Your answers to these questions will help you narrow your search as you decide where to apply.

Scenario: Steve Border
An Initial, School-Based,
One-to-One Interview

Chapter 1 Gathering Information

Chapter 2 Deciding Where to Apply

SCENARIO

STEVE BORDER

An Initial, School-Based, One-to-One Interview

Candidate:	Steve Border	
Interviewer:	Mr. Erickson	Principal

A graduate of large public schools, Steve is committed to working with students attending public schools in a large city. Enrolled in a graduate teacher education program in a major U.S. city, Steve is student teaching in a public elementary school cited for its innovative academic program and parental involvement. Although he has no hopes of landing a job in this setting, he expects to draw on his experiences here to find a good placement nearby.

Steve thought long and hard about where he could make the greatest contribution and where he would feel most comfortable. When choosing between public or private schools, Steve knew he wanted to work with students who attend public schools, specifically marginalized students. He also heard there were some schools with strong leadership, and then there were schools that no one seems to want to be in. Steve wants to teach in a school with a visionary leader. These early decisions in some ways narrowed the field for Steve as he pursued his teaching credential.

HOW DID STEVE GET AN INTERVIEW?

Steve has observed, volunteered, and student taught in a wide range of the schools available to residents in this city, which we call Newer City. As Steve participated in his teacher education program, he inquired about the criteria for including specific schools in the program, seeking to obtain a clearer understanding of the range of options available in the local schools. Steve wanted to get an accurate picture of the schooling situation, particularly the commitment to public education in Newer City, as he now sought to teach there. Won over by the students and faculty he worked with, as well as the wide array of low-cost resources available, Steve found living in Newer City was an attractive option.

Midway through his student teaching at the Performance School, he inquired about the possibility of a teaching position for the fall. Although neither his cooperating teacher nor the principal had any expectations of changes in the faculty or additional faculty lines, the principal, Ms. Taffel, indicated that she would see if she could find another school that might need a good new teacher. Steve impressed the principal with his resourcefulness and his dedication. Because she had informally observed him numerous times, she was in a position to recommend him to another principal. As luck would have it, Ms. Taffel located a possible school, the J. F. Kennedy School, and gave Steve the principal's name, Mr. Erickson, and the phone number.

At lunch that day, Steve called the J. F. Kennedy School with hopes of arranging an interview. Mr. Erickson was not available so Steve left a message including both his home phone number, and the fact that Ms. Taffel had suggested he call. Later that day, there was a message on Steve's voice mail from Mr. Erickson.

Steve returned the call the next morning at 7:30 a.m., hoping to make this contact before leaving for his student teaching responsibilities. To Steve's surprise, Mr. Erickson answered the phone himself but indicated this was a difficult time to talk and suggested that he visit the school next Thursday. Steve was particularly pleased with this appointment, considering he had sent out 20 letters and received no response.

HOW DID STEVE PREPARE FOR THE INTERVIEW?

Excited at having an interview scheduled, Steve asked his cooperating teacher, Ms. Norita, what he might be asked. Ms. Norita indicated that at her own interview, the principal, Ms. Taffel, had asked about her philosophy of teaching and particularly focused on her approaches to teaching reading and spelling. "And clearly I gave good answers," she said, "or I wouldn't be here now."

"How did you know what to say?" Steve asked.

"I think you need to answer from your heart. You can try to psych out the situation and figure out what the principal wants to hear. You want to be in a school where your philosophy is consistent with the principal's, or a place where the principal will allow you to do your own thing. I don't believe in playing a game to get a job because then you'll never know who you really are. As you know, I take my job seriously, and I think you do, too. So, I'd suggest that you want to be assigned to a school where your beliefs are respected and supported and where you will continue to learn. You clearly cannot learn everything in student teaching or in your teacher education program. I know that I'm constantly learning and loving it. You know that Ms. Taffel is so supportive of our looking at new programs and new ideas and she encourages us to try new ways to do things so that we can be even more effective than we are right now. I find those important qualities of my job. Perhaps you will want to consider similar concerns."

"Thanks. I guess I have a lot of thinking to do before I go for this interview," Steve said soberly.

When Steve got home, he checked to see where the J. F. Kennedy School was located on his map. The school was in a part of town that Steve rarely had reason to visit. He discovered that the J. F. Kennedy School was a newly constructed building in a fairly run-down part of the city where few of the students graduated from high school. Many of the parents were immigrants to this country, learning English along with their children. Those who were considered lucky worked long days under dismal conditions, and less fortunate ones were constantly seeking employment.

Steve was beginning to have second thoughts about this interview. From all he was learning, he was not sure he was prepared to teach in such a setting. He decided to visit the neighborhood of the school, both to learn how long it would take to get there and to get a read on whether he would feel comfortable there.

On Saturday morning, Steve mapped the travel plan from his apartment to the J. F. Kennedy School and started out on his bus trip. As he traveled from community to community, he became conscious of the differences in the storefronts, the quantity of merchandise that was displayed, and the number of people on the street corners. Gradually, as he approached the area where he thought the J. F. Kennedy School was located, he asked the woman seated next to him, "Do you know where the J. F. Kennedy School is?"

"Sure, my son goes to that school. Why do you ask?" she replied.

"Next week I have an interview for a teaching position there, and I wanted to find out exactly where the building is and how long it would take me to get there."

"I'll lead you there. I live just across the street from the school," she said. They got off the bus together. As they walked, the woman gave him a running commentary on the neighborhood, telling him where there was new construction and where he would want to avoid walking. Steve's guide brought him to the front entrance to the school.

"Thanks so much," Steve said.

"Good luck. I hope you get the job!"

As Steve approached the school he noticed an enthusiastic group of students counting to determine if everyone was there. He was impressed that they would arrange to meet on a Saturday for what looked like a school trip. When he noticed a couple of adults join the group, he approached one and introduced himself: "I'm Steve Border, and I've arranged an interview with Mr. Erickson for next Thursday for a position in the J. F. Kennedy School. Are you a teacher?"

"Yes, I teach most of these kids social studies and we're going to a museum today. How can I help you?"

"Do you like teaching at the Kennedy School? Do you think it's a good place to work?"

"I've been here for 3 years and I love it. But it's not the place for everyone."

"Why? Can you tell me a little more?" Steve asked.

"Well, I really don't have time, but briefly, you're totally on your own. There are so many things happening at the same time, so many kids around, and not enough adults to help them succeed. You need to be quite creative and resourceful. If you are, you'll have a wonderful time. If you are the type who needs or wants everybody to help you, and to tell you what to do, then this is not the place for you. The kids are wonderful. As you can see, I'm meeting with them on the weekend when most teachers are involved with friends and family. I have never been happier in my life. But I really need to get to my kids now. Sorry. I hope I get to see you again."

"Thanks a lot. I'll look forward to seeing you. Enjoy your museum visit."

Steve walked around the schoolyard and onto a quiet street lined with one- and two-family semiattached homes. He noticed that there were carefully tended gardens, which contrasted with the garbage strewn in the seemingly abandoned park next to the school.

Steve found a main street and then spotted the bus sign for his return trip. He was pleased with his serendipitous conversations on his trip and now knew it would take about 20 minutes to travel to the school on Thursday morning.

THE INTERVIEW

NOTES NOTES NOTES

On the day of the interview, as Steve approached the main entrance, a guard directed him to the principal's office. Mr. Erickson's secretary greeted him and asked him to take a seat. She announced over the public address system, "Mr. Erickson, please return to your office. Your appointment has arrived." Within 3 minutes Mr. Erickson appeared and extended his hand to Steve.

Mr. Erickson: Hi. I'm Mr. Erickson. So happy you could be here.

Steve: I'm Steve Border. I'm so happy to meet you.

Mr. Erickson: Please come in and have a seat. So tell me, why do you want to teach here at the Kennedy School?

Steve: Well, Ms. Norita and Ms. Taffel suggested that this might be a good place for me and I value their opinions. Also, I came over here on Saturday and saw some of your students and talked with one of your teachers. I really want to teach in this type of school. I attended these schools when I was younger and I think it's real important for students to succeed, especially marginalized students. [1]

Which comments communicate his desire to teach at Kennedy?

Mr. Erickson: Tell me a little about your experiences as a student teacher.

Steve: Well, I have been in several classrooms over the entire school year in two different schools, just five blocks apart. But there was a dramatic difference in the two placements. When I was at the Bleecker Street School, I was placed with a teacher who was getting ready to retire. She had worked with the third grade for the last 10 years, and she had all of her materials set, and she really only allowed me to do what she had planned.

Her lessons were easy to follow, which helped me gain confidence in the front of the classroom, but I never really had a chance to develop anything on my own. She worked mainly from the class sets of books in reading, math, and social studies. Science was delegated to a cluster teacher who came into the room when my cooperating teacher had a preparation period.

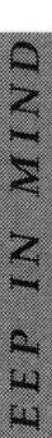

[1]Steve offers many reasons why he is considering the position, reminding the principal that he has been recommended for the job. His Saturday experience shows that Steve is really interested in knowing about the students and the school. He is clearly a serious candidate.

NOTES NOTES NOTES

At the beginning, I left the classroom during the science period with my cooperating teacher, but I realized that I could learn some different strategies from the science teacher. So, I worked along with her. At times she encouraged me to think up activities and projects for working with the class in small groups, just as she was doing. I learned so much about science and about small-group work. She also encouraged me to visit a few other classrooms where I was able to connect with teachers with different viewpoints and talk about using children's literature with the students, supplementing the basal reader, and sometimes integrating science with reading and writing.

When I went to the Performance School, I saw a totally different arrangement. My cooperating teacher was fairly new. She had only been teaching for 5 years. She had a lively classroom where the students were constantly working on different projects. I was able to eventually lead them in deciding on a new project. We established work groups to create a class guide to the neighborhood. We decided to include maps, photographs, and descriptions of all the resources available within a three-block radius of the school.

Steve has implicitly conveyed his philosophy of teaching in these comments. Note the key elements.

I've been working with a small group of students during this year, helping them to become more confident in their writing, and I've also been able to talk with teachers across several grades in our weekly team meetings. So I've had a very full experience, developing an understanding of how difficult it is to teach—but also how wonderful I feel about teaching. I really enjoy being with students—and talking with colleagues about our work together. [2]

Mr. Erickson: Have you read Chris Clark's book, *Thoughtful Teaching*? It sounds like you're talking about many of the practices that he's advocating.

Has Steve "blown it" by not knowing a book that Mr. Erickson asks about?

Steve: Actually, no, I don't think so.

But I have read other books that are helping me to understand the dynamics of the classroom. One that really inspires me is

---

KEEP IN MIND

[2]Steve emphasizes the range of settings he has experienced: teacher-directed activity and small-group learning. He wants to learn by visiting multiple teachers' classrooms. Steve is "professional" in that he does not mention teachers' names in situations that might be considered negative.

Steve is proud of his own work with his small group of students and in the team meetings with teacher colleagues. He shows enthusiasm for teaching. He also shows a long-term perspective on his career, considering a teacher with 5 years' experience fairly new.

NOTES NOTES NOTES

Shelley Harwayne's book. I can't remember the title right now, but it has helped me a lot. [3]

Mr. Erickson: What is the last book you read not assigned by your professors?

Steve: I really don't have a lot of time to read on my own, what with my student teaching, and my part-time job at Starbucks. I mainly read magazines and every day I read the newspaper. I can't remember the last book I picked up for my own enjoyment. There just doesn't seem to be time. [4]

Mr. Erickson: Why are you so anxious to get a job here? Why should we hire you?

Steve: As I said before, I've heard a lot of good things about your school from people whose opinions I respect, and I really enjoy teaching. On Saturday, I talked with a parent of one of your students, and a teacher, and I saw a group of your students. They all seemed enthusiastic about their experiences here. The kids all seemed so respectful and energetic that I feel I could work well with them. I also noticed that there was a small unused area where I might like to work with the students in creating a class—or a community garden—if we could get permission. I guess my juices are flowing with the possibility of teaching here, which means to me that I really will do a good job. [5]

KEEP IN MIND

[3]Steve honestly admits not knowing a particular book. His inability to remember the precise title suggests that he is not as prepared as he perhaps wants to be. Even though he did not know the title Mr. Erickson mentioned, Steve did mention a book that contributed to his knowledge, implying that he reads, remembers, and is developing a knowledge of professional literature.

[4]Mr. Erickson is trying to discover Steve's reading habits and the interests he will bring to his classroom. Steve's response affirms that he values reading and learning, including magazines and newspapers as part of his reading. Steve also suggests that once he gets a teaching position, he will have more time to read.

[5]Steve presents an upbeat, can-do, confident enthusiasm. He emphasizes that he took the time to come to the school in advance of the interview, and that he's thinking about what he might contribute to this specific school's resources. Steve might want to think about his use of the word *kids,* which some people consider disrespectful. Clearly Steve respects the children he has worked with, but he should make sure that he communicates that respect.

NOTES NOTES NOTES

How does Steve convey his knowledge of standards? What would you add to his response?

Mr. Erickson: You know we're all under a great deal of pressure to meet specific standards. If you were to get permission, how might your garden project help your students to meet the standards in, let's say, language arts? I suspect that you are familiar with the new standards?

Steve: Oh, yes. We've talked about them in my college courses, and I've gone to a couple of workshops on them as well. At this moment I can only talk generally, but when I'm actually doing my long-term planning, I would create a curriculum map—with the standards listed in one long column and the activities I would plan across the top. This map would help to guide my planning and would allow me to verify that I am actually attending to each of the standards.

Mr. Erickson: That sounds like a useful strategy. Perhaps, if you come here, you can share that organization with the other teachers. Tell me more about the connection between the garden and, let's say, the students' reading and writing? [6]

Steve: Sure. Let's take the issues of keeping track of which seeds are planted in each section of the garden, and knowing how to care for the different plants. I'd help the students to read the information provided on the seed packets, at first, helping them to learn some of the technical language of different zones where seeds grow best, for example. We'd need to verify that our geographic zone was included, by referring to maps, and then we'd need to create a system for making notes of what we had done, rotating the responsibilities. We'd keep journals, documenting the progress of the plants and the watering, fertilizing, and weeding that had been done. Students will simultaneously be creating useful documents while they are learning to access and interpret information accurately.

Mr. Erickson: That sounds pretty good. What makes you think you can handle our students?

Steve: I don't know, but I have confidence in my ability. I've had a lot of experience at the Performance School and as a leader of a group of kids connected with my church. I think I can work well

KEEP IN MIND

[6]From Mr. Erickson's response, clearly he wants more from Steve. He pushes further for additional information while commending Steve for having good strategies for organizing his planning. He also alludes to the possibility of collegial sharing, something Steve seems to have experienced earlier and valued.

Standards and curriculum mapping are brought up at many interviews. Steve should have been prepared to give some examples of activities that support a few standards.

with most kids. What can you tell me about your kids so that I can understand your concern for my handling them? [7]

Mr. Erickson: Perhaps you should do some substitute teaching here before the term is over so we can see how you function and you can see our students for yourself. Do you have any ideas of how you might go about organizing your classroom?

Steve: Well, I've not really thought about that a lot yet. But I will. Do you have some suggestions for me? [8]

Mr. Erickson: There are 40 teachers in this building and each teacher is different. I really want each classroom to reflect the individual personality of the teacher. We have very limited resources here. The textbooks are ordered by the School Board, and there are really no discretionary funds or wealthy parents to support our pet projects. So each teacher really needs to be very resourceful. Do you think you can fit into this environment? [9]

Steve: I'd sure like to try. I think I can be resourceful. I already know a lot about the museums and libraries and some parks and science laboratories we could get access to. I'll need to check out other resources. [10]

NOTES NOTES NOTES

What did Steve accomplish in his response?

How might you respond to this classroom management question?

What additional resources could you suggest?

KEEP IN MIND

[7]Steve suggests that his previous experiences will contribute to his success in this post. He asks for more information about "your kids," avoiding any snap judgments.

[8]We wonder why Steve has not given much thought to how he might organize his own classroom, because that seems like a reasonable question to expect. Perhaps Mr. Erickson's brief, direct question took Steve off guard. Steve might have posed a question to give himself time to think while Mr. Erickson talked. As an alternative analysis, perhaps Steve has been so involved in the day-to-day functioning of his student-teaching placements that he has not considered a long-range view of himself in the role of organizer.

[9]Mr. Erickson's response provides more information about the school as well as a clear sense of his leadership philosophy.

[10]Steve enumerates many of the local resources that might be incorporated into his classroom, implicitly informing Mr. Erickson of his knowledge of some of the community resources and his desire to draw on these in his curriculum. Steve's comment that he'll need to check out other resources suggests that he has much energy and a desire to discover all that is available for him to draw on.

Mr. Erickson: We traditionally have a fixed schedule for each day. Something like:

9:00–10:00	Reading
10:00–11:00	Social Studies
11:00–12:00	Math
12:00–12:30	Lunch
12:30–1:30	Music
1:30–2:30	Science
2:30–3:00	Writing

How would you respond to Mr. Erickson's question about the schedule?

Is this something you'd be happy with?

Steve: That seems somewhat like what I'm doing now at the Performance School. We have a regular schedule and the students know what to expect each day. They sometimes integrate writing and reading with the other subjects. Some of the teachers there seem to focus more on projects with the students incorporating math, science, and reading while they do their projects. I really like that integrated approach. Do you think it might be possible to mix some of these models?  [11]

Mr. Erickson: Anything is possible as long as the students learn. That's my policy. I have to run down to the yard now for the official start of the day. I really enjoyed meeting you and I'll get back to you when I know more about the positions that will be available at Kennedy. If you're interested in doing substitute teaching, leave your name and number with my secretary.

What do you think Steve infers from Mr. Erickson's statement, "Anything is possible as long as the students learn"?

Steve: Thanks so much for your time. [12]

KEEP IN MIND

[11]Steve is getting into a negotiating mode. He interprets the schedule that Mr. Erickson has at the Kennedy School as isolating reading and writing from the rest of the curriculum. He has seen this in some schools, but recently he has been integrating reading and writing while in the process of doing a project. Steve is trying to see, in one sense, if what Mr. Erickson said about each teacher's room being unique includes creating a unique schedule.

[12]Mr. Erickson, in reiterating his focus on student learning, has stated a clear leadership philosophy for Steve to consider. Mr. Erickson is clearly a hands-on principal, participating in the students' arrival at school. He efficiently calls an end to the conversation, leaving Steve with a very clear message: If you want to be seriously considered for a position at Kennedy, you will come back as a substitute teacher. Mr. Erickson has not offered Steve a job, but neither has he closed the door to him. In fact, Mr. Erickson has provided very clear information about his priorities, giving Steve the opportunity to buy into that value system and consider working at Kennedy or to look for a different placement.

WHAT DID STEVE DO WHEN HE LEFT THE INTERVIEW?

Steve could see that Mr. Erickson was under considerable time pressure, so he took leave of his office rapidly, stopping at the desk of Mr. Erickson's secretary to inquire about substitute teaching. After leaving his telephone number and an indication that he'd like to substitute teach, particularly in the fourth grade, he left the building. He made a mental note to send a letter of appreciation to Mr. Erickson, indicating that he would be interested in being considered for a position in the J. F. Kennedy School and he looked forward to the opportunity to substitute teach. Steve expected that Mr. Erickson would look in on his room during the substitute teaching days. In some respects, he might prefer this assessment of his teaching performance to the 15-minute demonstration lesson that one of his friends was required to do.

SUMMING UP

Steve is particularly pleased that he was able to convey that he CARES, a mnemonic and an acronym that he's created to make sure that he addresses his most important qualities:

C – Caring, cooperative
A – Altruistic
R – Resourceful, respectful
E – Energetic, enthusiastic
S – Serious

This school might be a great match for Steve. He seemed to get along well with Mr. Erickson, and there seemed to be an honest interaction going on, essential characteristics for a positive long-term professional relationship. Steve was enthusiastic, knowledgeable, and articulate in responding to Mr. Erickson's questions. He probably did not do as good a job of selling himself as he could have, however. He could have brought samples of his work at the Performance School. He clearly showed himself to be interested in the position, judging from his trip on Saturday and from his responses which connected his experiences to each question.

CHAPTER 1

GATHERING INFORMATION ABOUT POTENTIAL TEACHING POSITIONS

AT A GLANCE

In this space throughout the book, we provide an overview of each chapter's contents.

How will you find job openings? The more resourceful you are in seeking potential openings, the more likely you are to find an excellent place to teach. We offer information about schools and job openings from two sources: public announcements and personal networks.

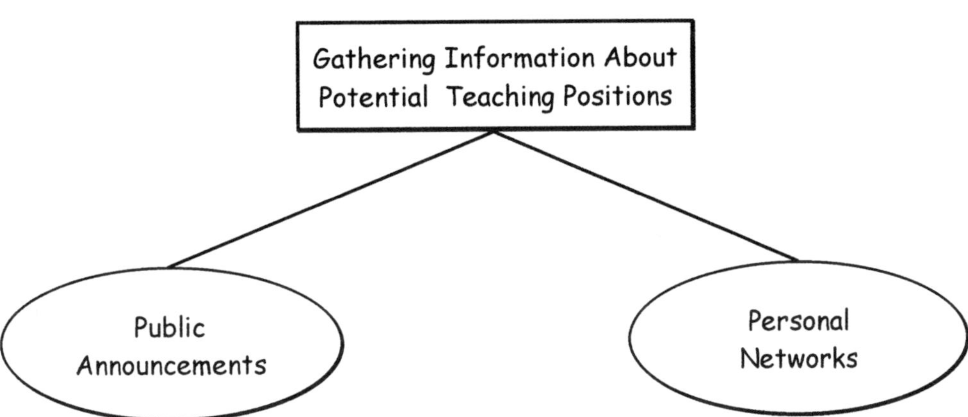

You are entering your job search at an opportune time. You are concerned with finding a school that will be best for *you*! As you gather information about a variety of schools, your criteria for what is best will become clearer and more apparent. How will you find the job openings? We have organized this chapter to respond to that question.

Many new teachers are simultaneously relocating to new communities, whereas others plan to remain fairly close to where they are completing their studies. The closer you are to the area where you plan to teach, the easier it is to access information about openings. Fortunately, however, in this electronic age, distance is no longer an obstacle.

You can find a great deal of information on the Internet, among other technological resources. You will discover that you are constantly gathering information in situations ranging from conversations with your cooperating teacher about how he or she found teaching positions, to talks with neighbors on line at the movies. You will need to find ways to evaluate the accuracy, currency, and comprehensiveness of information presented in all contexts. There are formal (public announcements) and informal (personal networks) means of advising about potential teaching posts.

PUBLIC ANNOUNCEMENTS

You will find information about potential openings in a wide range of settings, including newspapers, announcement boards, job fairs, Web sites, professional teaching agencies, university teacher placement offices, and statistical reports.

Newspaper advertisements attract the largest pool of potential candidates and enumerate a school's selection criteria. Some school districts advertise in local newspapers. These listings may be in the general employment section under "Educator," "Teacher," "Elementary Teacher," and "Social Studies Teacher," for example. They may also appear in a special Education section; for example, *The New York Times*'s Section 4, Week in Review, appears on Sunday, frequently listing teaching positions. National publications such as *Education Week* list jobs nationwide (see Fig. 1.1).

As you read the listings, you are likely to find phrasing that can be confusing. For now, if the newspaper is yours, cut out the ads, noting the source for future organization and reference. If you're reading the paper in the library, photocopy the appropriate pages. At this point we're focusing on accumulating information on potential openings. There are probably many abbreviations in the announcements that will be indecipherable at this

FIG. 1.1. Sample advertisements.

time. In chapter 2, we'll help you to interpret the language used in advertisements.

Identify two newspapers that will serve as initial resources and note the headings under which each newspaper posts openings.

Announcement boards are typical repositories for fliers listing job openings and announcing job fairs sent to schools, colleges, and universities. These boards are typically located in a school's main office, in a teachers' lounge, outside college departmental

NOTES NOTES NOTES

offices, or within the career placement office. Make a point of regularly checking the bulletin boards in your school and the schools you visit. Because the posted materials are frequently reviewed by many people, they may be haphazardly organized. If you systematically review each paper, you may find a wonderful job underneath some outdated materials. Be a good detective.

Note the locations of two announcement boards in your school.

Job fairs are sponsored by teacher centers and school districts. Typically these fairs are announced in newspaper advertisements, in fliers posted on college and school bulletin boards, and at professional conferences. Sometimes they are addressed to a specific audience, such as minorities, new teachers, or recently retired teachers. Keep your eyes open for these opportunities.

Candidates are encouraged to bring several copies of their résumé to leave with school representatives. Descriptive brochures, video clips, fliers, and posters usually highlight the district's assets. Initial screening interviews and informal conversations provide detailed information about openings. In a short time you are able to gather a great deal of information and have numerous, although brief, interviews.

Locate at least one upcoming job fair in your area. Create a calendar to note future job fairs in your area.

Web sites list information from school districts and state education departments. Check the Web site of the Clearinghouse on Elementary and Early Childhood Education at http://ericps.ed.uiuc.edu/eece/statlink.html. Figure 1.2 helps you to access the 50 state Departments of Education and Fig. 1.3 displays sample home pages of individual state education departments.

There are numerous Internet sites that list job openings from across the nation and around the world. Some Web sites forward your résumé and teaching application to member schools. For example, a regional education partnership established an "Online Teacher Application System" for candidates to apply for teaching positions in 47 geographically linked school districts. New regional consortiums are being created, with *Education Week* recently announcing a national database. Most recently, the U.S. Department of Education announced the launching of the National Teacher Recruitment Clearinghouse, posting information on teaching opportunities across the nation, in addition to links created by school districts, state education departments, and teacher-recruitment programs. The clearinghouse is online at www.recruitingteachers.org.

There are several Web sites that offer Listservs (sometimes called mail rings) targeting specific groups of teachers. Separate rings are available for districts to post openings.

Some Web sites enable you to learn about employment trends, salary ranges, the cost of living, cultural activities, and educational facilities. Real estate agencies and local newspapers frequently post school and neighborhood information. Other sites may offer ideas on writing effective résumés. Daily, there are

Educational Resources on the Internet

State Departments of Education

Click on the image map or the text links below to link to a particular state's Department of Education or similar organization.

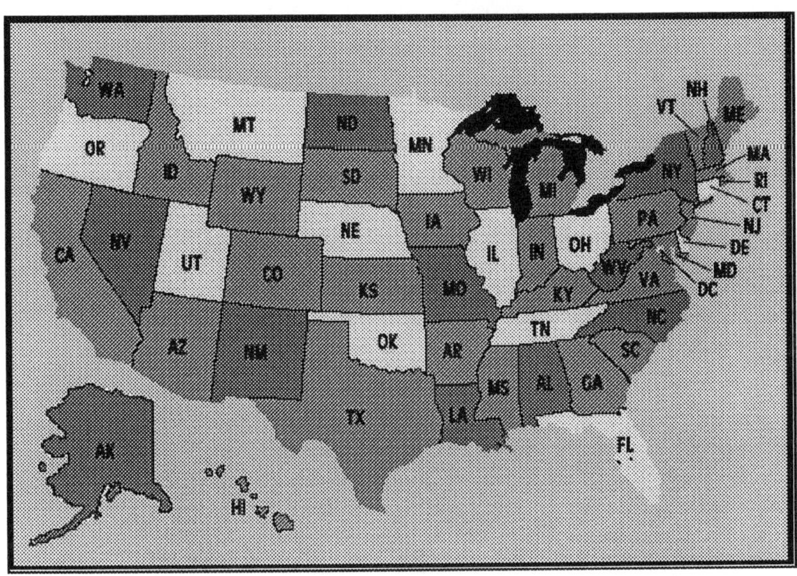

Alabama
Alaska
Arizona
Arkansas
California
Colorado
Connecticut
Delaware
District of Columbia
Florida
Georgia
Hawaii
Idaho
Illinois
Indiana
Iowa
Kansas

Kentucky
Louisiana
Maine
Maryland
Massachusetts
Michigan
Minnesota
Mississippi
Missouri
Montana
Nebraska
Nevada
New Hampshire
New Jersey
New Mexico
New York
North Carolina

North Dakota
Ohio
Oklahoma
Oregon
Pennsylvania
Rhode Island
South Carolina
South Dakota
Tennessee
Texas
Utah
Vermont
Virginia
Washington
West Virginia
Wisconsin
Wyoming

FIG. 1.2. Links to state departments of education.

new Web sites being launched. Be creative and expansive in your electronic searches.

Search for potentially useful Web sites and note their locations. Bookmark or add these to your list of favorite sites on your computer.

Professional placement agencies may be useful. Recruiting New Teachers is a national organization with a mission to expand the representation of a broader range of cultures and experiences in the teaching profession. They identify teaching positions for new teachers and list candidates' qualifications in their database, which is available to member districts nationally.

FIG. 1.3. Sample home pages of state departments of education.

Note on the blank pages throughout the book the names, addresses, telephone numbers, e-mail addresses, and fax numbers of local teacher placement agencies for future reference.

There are a number of teacher placement agencies that will assist you in finding a position. Schools and districts list openings with these agencies, hoping to access a greater number of candidates for their posts. Frequently these agencies advertise in the employment pages of the local newspapers, typically charging a fee for their services. They may assist you with interview strategies as well as critique your résumé.

University teacher placement offices are repositories of a wealth of information. Your university or college probably has a career planning and placement office. This center typically lists teaching opportunities and offers workshops on job finding. Lists of openings are updated periodically. You may request these lists by mail or connect to a Listserv for updates. Other services typically offered through the career placement office are addressed in chapter 4.

Search/Find

- Locate the site of your school's placement office.
- Note the hours of operation.
- Note the names of the counselor(s).
- Visit the placement office to obtain copies of all documents and resources available.

Statistical reports published by the federal government's National Center for Education Statistics report on staffing trends, achievement scores, budget allocations, enrollment trends, class size, average length of teacher service, and certification status. These data, accessible through the Internet, offer you the opportunity to find districts that are likely to need teachers with your qualifications. For example, in a district or region with a teacher population averaging more than 25 years of experience, there may be the expectation of a significant number of retirements.

Reports on student achievement, including scores from tests administered by the state education department, may be read online, downloaded, or ordered in paper format. Commercial organizations publish guides that compare schools and school districts on many characteristics. You may want to look at published comparisons when making your own assessments.

Search/Find
Using the Internet, access the education statistics for a school district near your residence. Note the numbers of teachers employed and students enrolled.

Directories of public schools, independent schools, and religiously affiliated schools are published by local and national professional organizations and unions. Names of principals and other administrators, telephone numbers, and addresses of public and private schools are available from the Department of Education in each state.

Check telephone directories for listings of public schools. These are typically listed within the governmental listings under "Education." For private schools, check the private school directories stored at the reference desk of your local library to note the address and the principal's name.

Search/Find
Visit your college and local libraries.

Identify titles of potentially relevant directories, noting the call numbers or Web addresses for future referral.

Search/Find
List two school sites you might visit, noting the following contact information from a directory:

School Name	Address	Principal's Name	Phone No.	Secretary's Name

NOTES NOTES NOTES

PERSONAL NETWORKS

Published sources provide important information, but informal sources—the proverbial grapevine—also provide a totally different perspective. Informal networks are often valuable in finding a teaching position. You need to network by informing as many people as possible that you are looking for a job. Do not be shy about it. Be creative in your approach as you (a) visit schools, (b) make personal contacts, (c) sustain professional contacts, and (d) read local newspapers.

School visits provide excellent opportunities to explore the differences among school cultures. All schools are supposed to be good places for students to learn. However, from Kozol's (2000) *Ordinary Resurrections* and Anyon's (1997) *Ghetto Schooling,* we know this is not the case. New teachers are frequently employed in schools from which experienced teachers seek transfers. These schools are typically populated by highly mobile students whose parents have limited confidence communicating in schools. The dearth of available instructional materials frequently matches students' limited experiences with success in school.

During Open School Week and other events open to the community, take the opportunity to visit classrooms, view student work, and obtain a sense of the professional climate in a range of schools that interest you. Familiarity with the larger school community can be useful when you are identifying schools to apply to and when explaining your reasons for applying to the school during your interview. As you visit different neighborhoods, indicate to the school secretary or administrative assistant your interest in teaching there and leave a copy of your résumé.

NOTES NOTES NOTES

Frequently the secretarial staff is helpful in pinpointing available positions. Assistance from these individuals will usually serve you well. Make sure you maintain contact with any schools that really impress you. Sometimes volunteering to work at a school allows the staff to get to know you, and they may find a way to keep good workers. Be cautious of becoming a pest, though!

Some districts will only hire teachers who served as teacher assistants or substitute teachers in the district. Other districts have a policy or practice of not hiring their teacher assistants. Some schools may prefer to appoint new teachers whose salaries are less costly than experienced ones. Some may prefer to hire experienced teachers. It is essential for you to find out what the local policy and practices are. The information may be available from teachers in the district, from the school secretarial staff, from the teacher organization, or from the Board of Education.

Personal contacts are a very valuable asset. Networking is a generally respected activity in the business world; it is equally appropriate in education. Although not looking for special treatment, you want to find a way to be seriously considered. Be direct in asking for assistance.

Tell friends and relatives that you are looking for a job and ask if they know anyone who might help. Remind them how close you are to achieving certification. They may know about unadvertised openings. Continue to announce your interest in every conversation. You never know when a new position will be advertised or a person will connect your availability with a new posting on a bulletin board. In conversations with friends and colleagues, school district personnel may mention that there will be an opening.

There is a thin line between using your contacts and abusing your contacts. If you have an ongoing relationship with a person who may have access to relevant information, you are being professional and savvy when you ask for help in gathering information or checking on the progress of your application. If you create a relationship with the ulterior motive of being recommended, you are being abusive. This strategy may be effective once, but you may develop a reputation for "using" people.

Search/Find

Make a list of some of the people you may be able to contact on a personal level, including their telephone numbers or e-mail contacts. (Be sure to include your postal delivery person, your friend from camp, your aunt's friend, etc.)

Name	Contact Information

Professional contacts may be more valuable than personal contacts. As you engage in conversations with your professors, your field specialists and supervisors, and your cooperating teachers, ask them how to go about getting a job and whether they know of any openings. They may offer some specific information about how they got their jobs and about the interviewing process. These conversations enable your potential references to offer a current recommendation for you. Be sure to get permission to use the person's name as a reference before you offer it to a potential employer.

Search/Find

List the names of a few people with whom you've established a positive professional relationship and the most efficient way for you to contact them. Continue to add to this list throughout your professional career.

Name	Contact Information

Local newspapers may report the planned opening of a new school or the expansion of an existing school. You may discover a new housing development has opened or a school is overcrowded. This information should be added to your growing file of leads and should be explored as soon as possible.

SUMMING UP

You are probably amazed at all the potential resources to access information about teaching using public and personal sources. Now is the time to initiate your research and gather leads on possible job openings. Be sure to collect and read a wide range of advertisements and postings to get the most out of chapter 2.

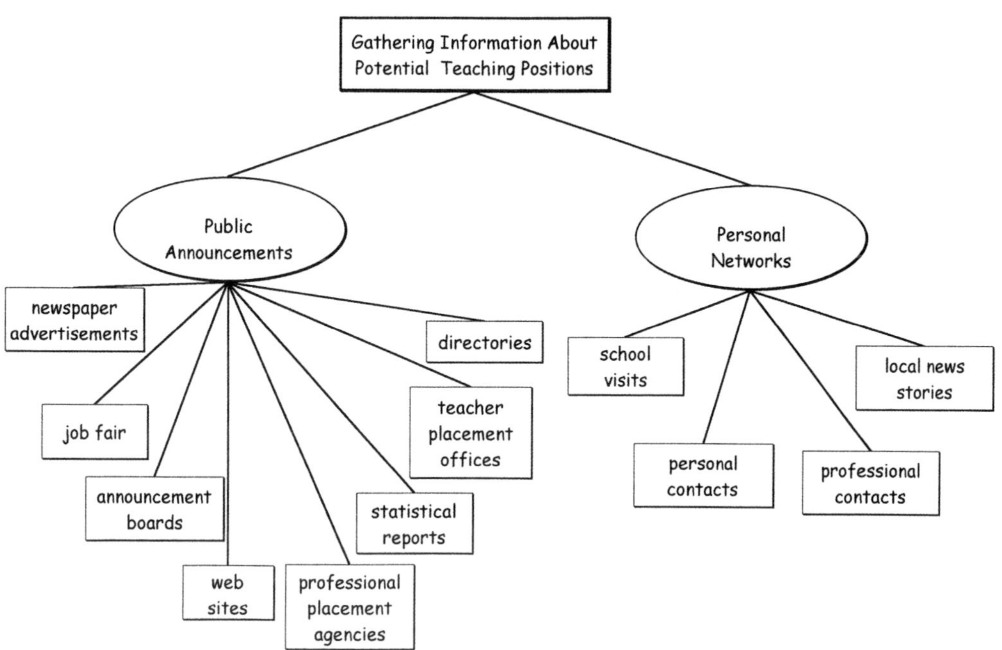

CHAPTER 2 DECIDING WHERE TO APPLY

AT A GLANCE

In this chapter we consider your personal preferences and those enumerated by schools. Personally you will need to contemplate a wide array of options. We provide a series of decision trees to organize this process for you. Schools also have preferences that are frequently communicated in their announcements of positions. You will examine your preferences in light of these diverse prospects.

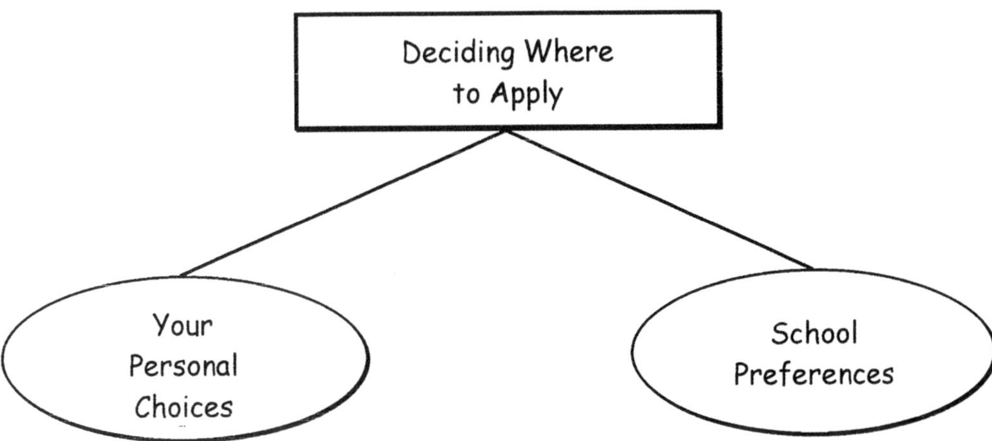

"Where should I send my résumé?"

"Is this district for me?"

These are overlapping questions. When beginning a job search, the appropriateness of schools and districts is of primary concern to a candidate. In areas where there are numerous openings, target a subset of these opportunities. In areas with few openings, candidates frequently "blanket" the community with résumés. There are many reasons to question the value of this. When you send out numerous letters indiscriminately, you are likely to find:

1. You have no time to follow up when you have so many résumés out there.

2. You have no knowledge of the unique qualities of the district if and when you are called for an interview.

3. A generic letter omits a connection between your background and the school's needs.

4. A generic letter suggests that you are not really interested in this specific school, but rather just want a job, any job.

Openings occur throughout the academic year. It may be advantageous to start with a class at the beginning of the school year, but it is not unusual, particularly for new teachers, to be offered a position once the term has begun, a somewhat reassuring phenomenon.

Given the opportunity to consider teaching "anywhere," you are likely to feel overwhelmed at the magnitude of your choices. Monitoring and promoting your applications in each school are time-consuming processes. You need to carefully consider the school(s) you want to pursue and limit the number of applications you initiate and follow up on. Schools also have preferences that will limit your choices. In this chapter we help you consider ways to narrow your choices.

YOUR PERSONAL CHOICES

Although there are many similarities among schools, there are also important distinguishing characteristics, some of which may be useful in identifying the places where you'll be most comfortable and successful. Your considerations will include many factors, such as geographic locations, sources of funding, responsibilities, assignments, grade levels, school structures, and the unique qualities of the school.

In each of the following sections, you'll find decision trees and tables serving to graphically represent the choices you have. Use the empty boxes to note any personally important characteristics. Circle your choices as you consider your options. You may include multiple options as preliminary choices (e.g., tenure track, leave replacement, and immediate opening). You can—and will—revise these choices, but the exercise of making choices is an important part of your search.

Table 2.1 presents some of the choices you will need to ponder, keeping in mind these are not necessarily mutually exclusive choices. As you visualize teaching in your ideal placement, ask yourself, "What are the characteristics of that setting?" Identifying your ideal will guide you in deciding those compromises you are willing to make to get a position. Because there is no perfect placement, you will either ultimately create the ideal setting wherever you are placed or you will continue to search for a more compatible setting.

Steve used Table 2.1 as a reference to document his ideal position (see Table 2.2). His circles tell us his ideal position is in a local public school as a full-time, tenure-track, K–4 generalist, interdisciplinary teacher. In the last column he added a school characteristic that is especially important to him, professional learning community. He wants to be in a setting where he will continue to learn about teaching while helping his students become better learners. Your ideal choices and Steve's certainly will differ.

In contrast to Steve's ideal position, there are additional markings in Table 2.3. The choices Steve has circled show he is willing to consider any type of opening (anticipated, leave replacement, immediate opening, and tenure track). In addition, he is willing to consider positions as an assistant teacher or a substitute teacher on a full-time or long-term basis. Steve is flexible in some ways, considering additional alternatives beyond his ideal setting to broaden his search. We note that he is still not willing to relocate, nor will he consider a private or independent school placement.

Now that we've looked at Steve's ideal position and contrasted it with the greater range of positions he's willing to consider, it's time for us to help you go through that process as well. Let's focus on each of these choices individually as we contemplate each option in greater detail.

Geographic limitations quickly reduce your many options, helping to provide a clearer focus for your search. Perhaps the first major decision you will make is whether to teach in the United States or in another country. Because the application

Table 2.1 My Ideal Position

ISSUES	Geography	Funding	Length & Type	Title	Assignment	Grade(s)	Specialization(s)	School Characteristics
CHOICES	Local	Public	Anticipated vacancy	Teacher	Full-time	Pre-K	Generalist	
	Relocate	Private/independent	Leave replacement	Assistant teacher	Part-time	K–4	Content specialist	
		Combined private and public	Immediate opening	Substitute teacher	Long-term substitute	Middle school	Interdisciplinary	
			Tenure-track		Per diem substitute	High school	Reading/literacy	
							Family & careers	
							Gifted	
							Special education	

Table 2.2 Steve's Ideal Position

ISSUES	Geography	Funding	Length & Type	Title	Assignment	Grade(s)	Specialization(s)	School Characteristics
CHOICES	(Local)	(Public)	Anticipated vacancy	(Teacher)	(Full-time)	Pre-K	(Generalist)	*Professional learning community*
	Relocate	Private/independent	Leave replacement	Assistant teacher	Part-time	(K–4)	Content specialist	
		Combined private and public	Immediate opening	Substitute teacher	Long-term substitute	Middle school	(Interdisciplinary)	
			(Tenure-track)		Per diem substitute	High school	Reading/literacy	
							Family & careers	
							Gifted	
							Special education	

Table 2.3 Steve's "Willing to Consider" Choices

ISSUES	Geography	Funding	Length & Type	Title	Assignment	Grade(s)	Specialization(s)	School Characteristics
CHOICES	Local	Public	Anticipated vacancy	Teacher	Full-time	Pre-K	Generalist	*Professional learning community*
	Relocate	Private/independent	Leave replacement	Assistant teacher	Part-time	K–4	Content specialist	
		Combined private and public	Immediate opening		Long-term substitute	Middle school	Interdisciplinary	
			Tenure-track		Per diem substitute	High school	Reading/literacy	
							Family & careers	
							Gifted	
							Special education	

procedures and expectations are so dramatically different between these two settings, you will need to decide this issue first. Within this book we provide extensive information about locating positions in the United States. If you are considering teaching outside of the United States, you may consider teaching in American schools abroad. Because each country has unique procedures you will need to access additional sources. Valuable resources that may facilitate your local or international search are noted at the end of this chapter.

NOTES NOTES NOTES

The next geographic issue is deciding whether to stay close to where you are currently living or to relocate. Part of this decision might be influenced by personal plans, but other factors may also come into play. There are sections of our country where there are abundant teaching positions, and others where there are limited opportunities. If you are contemplating a move, you might want to select a community where there are likely to be positions that align with your needs and interests. Note your current thinking in Fig. 2.1.

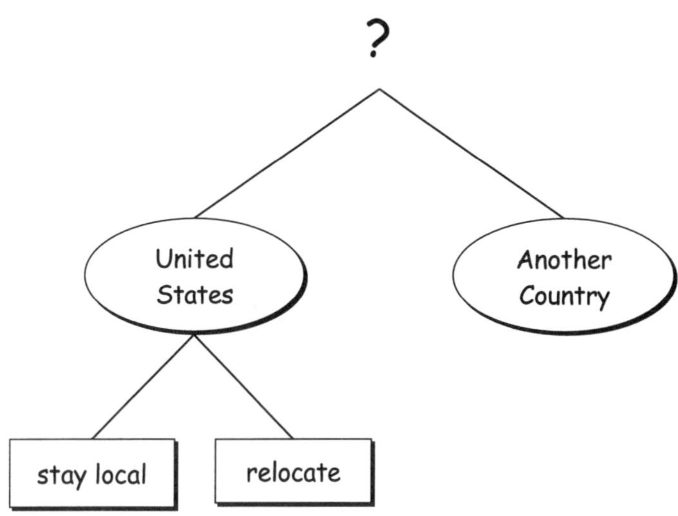

FIG. 2.1. Decision 1: Geographic location.

School funding sources—more commonly looked on as "Who pays for this school?"—typically distinguish school cultures. You will need to consider whether you want to teach in a school that is funded by the government (public school) or in one funded by student tuition (private or independent school). School climates, priorities, and organizations in these two settings may differ so that a person is more comfortable in one than the other.

Ideally all teachers are accountable to their students and to their own professional ethics. Tenure-track positions are offered in public schools, but they are less likely to be available in private schools. With recent moves to offer alternatives within public schools, some profit-making organizations are contracting with public schools to provide services, blurring the distinction between public and independent school. With this trendsetting practice, it becomes essential that you research the specific regulations and expectations at each site.

Public schools (whether they are named Public School 6, Beacon Charter School, or Cascades Center for Learning) are part of a larger system—a school district. Some of these are called union free school districts, community school districts, or the Board of Education of the City of X.

Public schools frequently use numbers to name the schools, thus we read about P.S. 77 (Public School No. 77), or CES 77 (Community Elementary School No. 77). Some nomenclature included in advertisements and job listings makes it easier to identify public schools, for example:

Community School District No. 2 (CSD 2)
Community School No. 115 (CS 115)
Union Free School District (UFSD)
Board of Education (BOE; Bd. of Ed.)
Public School (P.S. 86)
Charter School
Alternative School

Charter schools and alternative schools are publicly funded schools established to expand the educational options offered in the district. They are typically smaller in size with a clear philosophical or theme-based focus. Charter schools are directly responsible to the state agency that both charters them and funds them. They may have different recruitment policies and requirements than other public schools. The faculty in the public schools are mainly accountable to local taxpayers, parents, the students, and the administration of their school.

The title of public school indicates the school is attended by residents in the local region and funded mainly by tax revenue from residents and businesses in the town, village, or city. Some public school districts have negotiated teaching contracts with unions or professional organizations. These contracts (establishing the salary schedule and other working conditions) are binding on both the district and the teachers who work there. In some districts, teachers are free to select the school(s) to which they will apply. In others, there are explicit limitations on teachers' options. You will want to investigate their hiring and reappointment policies as well as the range of educational program offerings.

Private (or independent) schools (in contrast to public schools) are smaller in size and independent in establishing working conditions. Student enrollment in private schools is usually selective; frequently students and their parents are interviewed and assessed for their "goodness of fit" with the institution using various criteria, including standardized test scores. Students who attend these schools may pay tuition or may receive tuition assistance in the form of vouchers or scholarships.

The curriculum offered, the tests students take, and the professional backgrounds of the faculty in independent schools may differ from those mandated for public schools. Often, teacher certification requirements established by the state have no impact on an independent school's criteria for appointing faculty.

The faculty in private schools are principally accountable to the parents who pay the tuition dollars as well as the administration of the school. Labels that distinguish private schools include independent, college preparatory, and religiously affiliated. Some religiously affiliated schools seek candidates who will teach religion classes. Note your choices in Fig. 2.2. Once you've made the decision between public and independent schools, there are still more choices for you to consider.

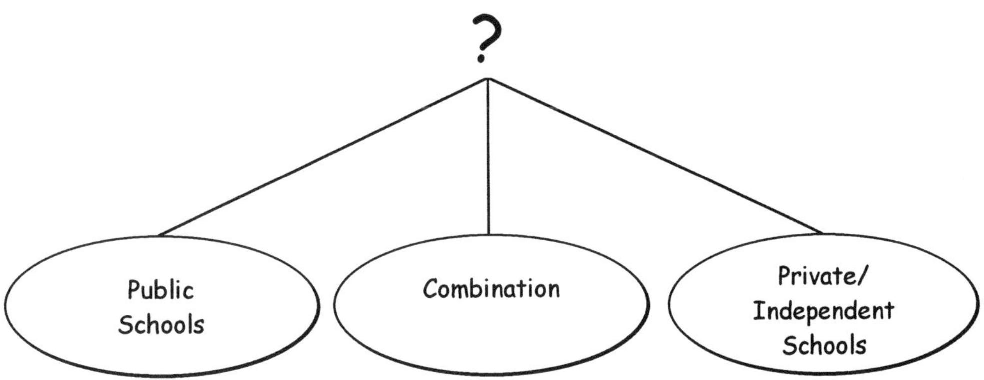

FIG. 2.2. Decision 2: Funding sources.

The types of positions available for your consideration are diverse in many dimensions. Some job listings and advertisements will note that there is an immediate opening, a firm opening, or that the position is available. These terms contrast with advertisements noting an anticipated position, suggesting that a retirement is expected or the school leader has requested authority to create a new position; official commitment is anticipated. The listing is posted in good faith that the funding will be forthcoming, but there are no guarantees. The district or school is warning candidates that it's possible the position may not be funded, in which case the search will be terminated. Some candidates may decide not to pursue openings that are only tentative. As a neophyte seeking to get a position, you may dismiss this potential occurrence and adopt an optimistic stance.

APPLY! APPLY! APPLY!

NOTES NOTES NOTES

You will notice that some positions are designated tenure-track, or probationary teacher, or pretenure teacher (see Fig. 2.3). These terms all imply that the position is expected to be a long-term position that may eventually (after 3–7 years of satisfactory teaching evaluations) result in the granting of tenure. The issues of tenure are multifaceted, complex, and varied. Your cooperating teacher and other educational colleagues may have valuable information regarding local tenure policies. Be aware of schools where successful teachers are rarely awarded tenure.

Listings that identify the position as a leave replacement, 1-year family leave replacement, or a fall leave medical replacement are temporary positions with finite beginnings and endings, sometimes considered "permanent substitute" posts. Some applicants choose these positions because they like the schools and hope that the school will find a way to place them in a tenure-track opening when the initial temporary appointment ends. Other candidates, seeking to explore a variety of schools or to avoid a long-term commitment, prefer temporary assignments. Even if there are no openings in the school after the temporary position ends, the acquisition of 1 year's experience and a laudatory recommendation may jump-start your subsequent search. Circle your choices in Fig. 2.3.

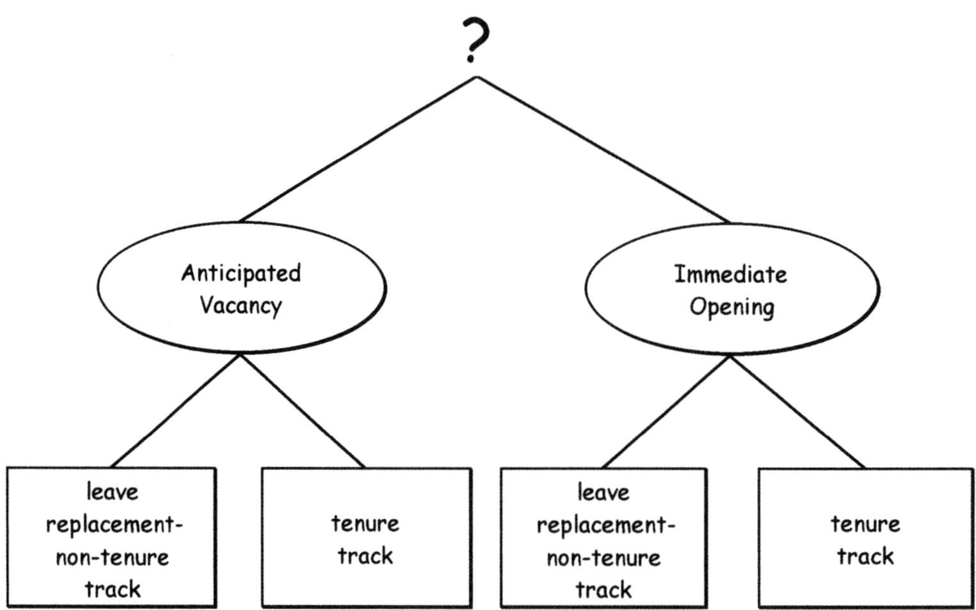

FIG. 2.3. Decision 3: Types of positions available.

Teaching responsibilities vary across schools. Schools employ people with a variety of titles, including head teacher, teacher, teaching assistant, and substitute teacher. As you visit schools, you may become familiar with additional titles given to people who work at the school. An opportunity to apply for such positions may be offered to you. It is important to know the responsibilities of those positions when considering where to apply. Because the responsibilities may vary across districts, it is important to investigate the opportunity and determine if it is likely to be attractive to you, tapping your knowledge and strengths.

Teachers typically have full responsibility for the classroom, whereas assistants work under the guidance and supervision of a teacher. Districts often employ newly certified teachers as teaching assistants, a prerequisite to considering them to fill full-time teaching posts. Teaching assistants typically have fewer responsibilities and receive lower salaries as they become increasingly knowledgeable and proficient as teachers.

Substitute teaching positions may be as short as 1 day in duration, or they may last for months. Schools maintain lists of approved persons to call on a per-diem (daily) basis to fill in for an absent teacher. When teachers take a leave of absence for health reasons, or to provide child care, for example, a long-term substitute may be assigned. Beginning teachers frequently start in this capacity as a temporary measure while continuing to search for a full-time post. New teachers, particularly those assigned after the start of the semester may be classified as permanent substitutes. (This is a fascinating contradiction in terms emblematic of many school practices. See *Enduring Schools* [Brause, 1992] for more insights into these anomalies.)

Openings may be for a full-time teacher, part-time teacher, or occasional teacher. Teacher titles may also include head teacher, grade leader, teacher specialist, or itinerant teacher. A head teacher or grade leader may be expected to lead a group of teachers at the same grade level. A specialist teacher may work with several classes on a regular basis, sharing professional expertise in a specific domain such as science, social studies, literacy, food preparation, or anthropology. An itinerant teacher travels from one school to another or from one home to another. Teachers with dual assignments have responsibilities for two areas (e.g., reading and science).

In addition to a coterie of full-time professionals, schools frequently employ part-timers. These part-timers supplement the regular staff's expertise, providing additional support to the educational program. Part-time teachers may be listed as P/T, or .4 Art, .2 Remedial Reading, 3 days/week; 25 hours; or a.m. only. In these contexts, a .4 Art teacher may be assigned 40% of a full week's schedule, an assignment for 2 days per week or 2 hours per day, for example. In other contexts, a part-time teacher also may be called per diem, or temporary. Typically these positions are not tenure-track positions, and frequently do not include health benefits, but they do give you access to the school's culture. Some school districts package several part-time positions among several schools in the district, thereby creating a full-time, itinerant position, whereas others seek to keep each specialization distinct. Review the decision tree in Fig. 2.4 as you consider your ideal choices.

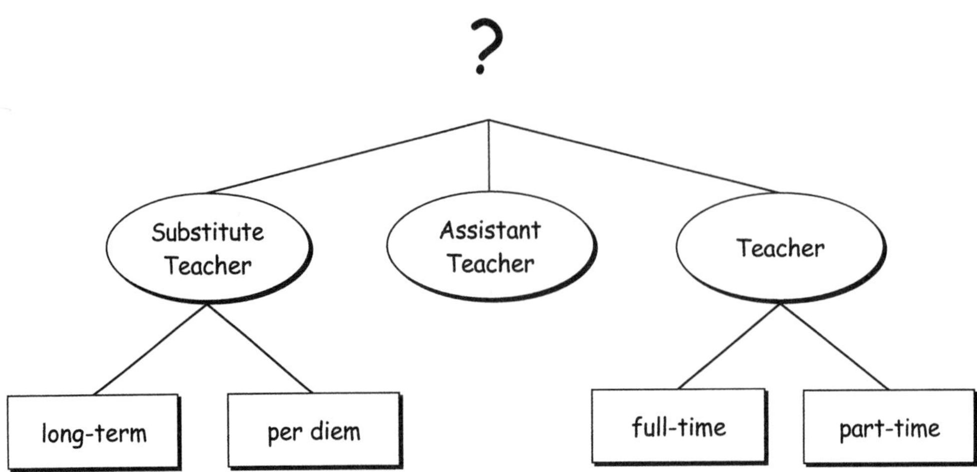

FIG. 2.4. Decision 4: Teaching responsibilities.

Grade-level organizations stratify students according to age, academic achievement, interest, or subject disciplines. Each elementary school, for example, may have students who are 7 years of age, but the organization in the school is not as predictable (see Table 2.4). New teachers are usually appointed to fit into the existing structure. The organizational features are usually noted in the listing (e.g., kindergarten, elementary).

You may find K–6 schools, primary or early childhood centers, intermediate schools, middle schools, junior high schools, and high schools. The specific grade range within each structure is determined locally. Alternative schools often experiment with different organizational structures, such as multiage grouping or looping in which the teacher stays with the same group of students for multiple years. The organization distinguishing one school from another is based on the number of students enrolled, the available space in each school building, and implicit teaching and learning philosophies.

Each school seeks specialists in different areas, helping to identify the unique qualities of each institution. Most schools organize themselves by grade level, single grades, or combinations (see Figs. 2.5 and 2.6 for organizational structures). By identifying your own strengths along with your area(s) of certification, you will be able to choose the schools that are seeking teachers with your expertise.

Some common terms and abbreviations used by districts in advertising may be in shorthand and need explanation. We offer generic descriptions; it is essential that you discover the unique

Table 2.4 Typical School Structures

Typical School Labels	Possible Grade Levels
Early childhood center	Pre-K- 2; or K for whole district
Lower school	Pre-K–6
Primary	Pre-K–3
Elementary	K–6, K–5, K–4
Intermediate	3–6, 3–5, 4–6
Upper school	7–12
Middle school	5–8, 5–7, 6–8, 7-8
Junior high school	6–9, 6–8, 7–9
Senior high school	8–12, 9–12, 10–12

characteristics of each setting that you consider. Additional information will be available at the school or district itself. Evidence of state teaching certification may be expected in designated areas.

Elem./Bil. An opening for a teacher who is knowledgeable about bilingual education focusing on students in elementary grades. It is not clear if this is a pull-out position, where children are removed for short blocks of time from their classroom, or if the assignment is as a bilingual classroom teacher for an unidentified grade or for multiple grades.

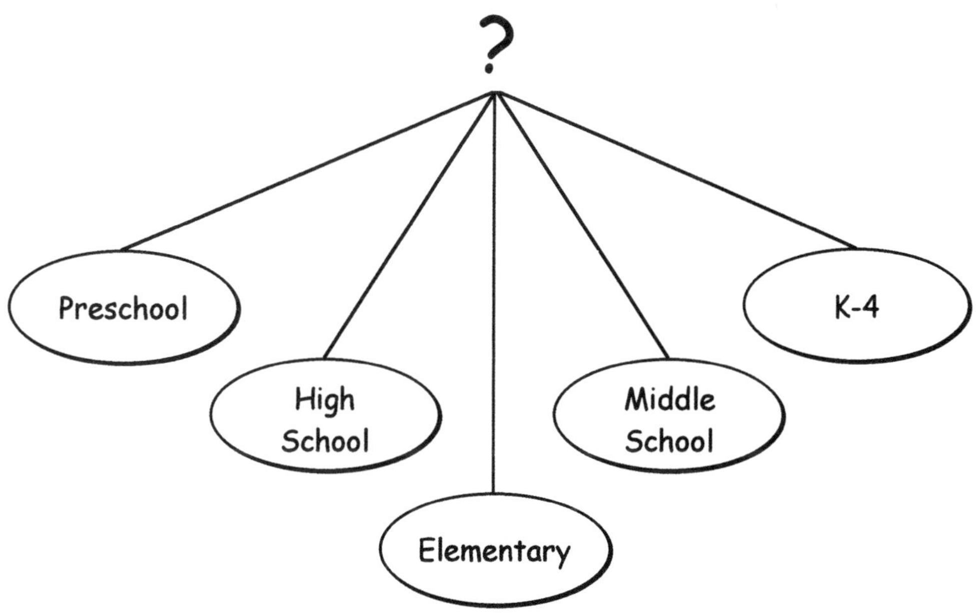

FIG. 2.5. Decision 5: Grade level.

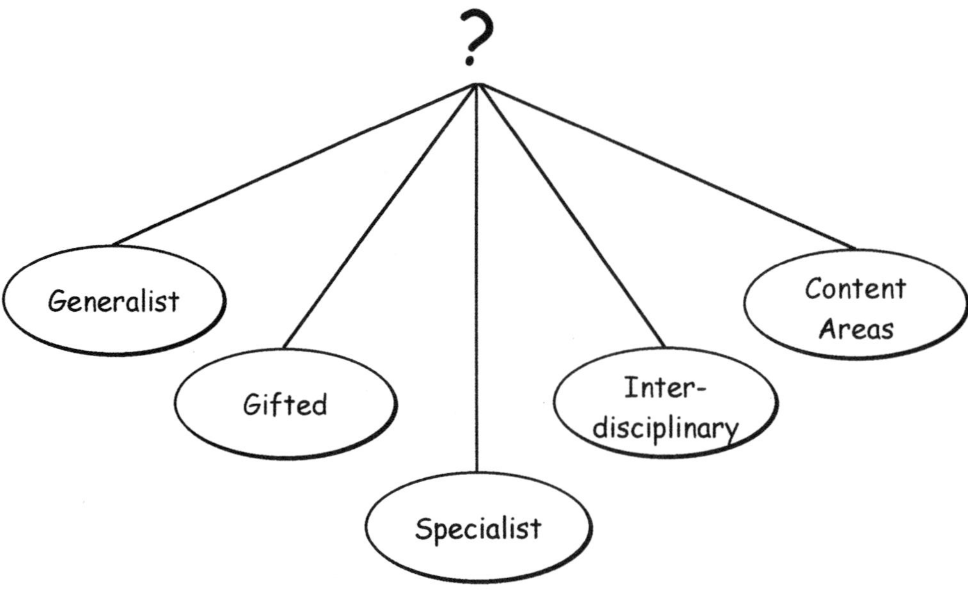

FIG. 2.6. Decision 6: Specializations.

Elem./M.S. A placement in elementary and/or middle school.

Elem. Rdg. A person qualified to teach reading in the elementary grades, probably working with students at a variety of grade levels, or perhaps as part of a pull-out or push-in program, where the reading teacher participates along with the regular classroom teacher.

Enrichment A term used to designate a teacher who typically adds to the existing curriculum—for a select group of students or for whole classes. This may be in a pull-out program or it may be in collaboration with the regular teacher in the class. It may include working with several groups of students and several teachers.

ESL/Rdg. A teacher who is knowledgeable about teaching English as a Second Language (also called English language learners) as well as developing students' reading competencies.

4th/5th Grade A teacher who will work in a combined class of fourth- and fifth-grade students.

Grades K–4 One position in which students ranging in grade placement from kindergarten through Grade 4 will be in the same room. Alternatively, perhaps multiple teachers are being sought for all the grade levels in this grouping. This confusion may be clarified by the placement in parentheses of a number (e.g., 4 positions).

Gr. 6 - L.A./Rdg. A person to teach sixth-grade language arts and reading, probably to multiple groups of students, perhaps in a departmentalized setting.

LA/SS A dual focus on social studies and language arts, perhaps as an integrated curriculum, or perhaps as separate subjects.

LD/ED Elementary A teacher qualified to teach elementary grade students designated as learning disabled or emotionally disabled.

P.E./H.S./M.S. PE stands for physical education, HS for high school, and MS for middle school. The assignment may be in two buildings.

Sp.Ed.-El. A specialist in special education, specifically on the elementary level.

Each school has unique characteristics that you will want to identify. You may infer a great deal of information from the descriptions offered by the school. Some phrases incorporated into advertisements focus on different aspects of import to the school and they are potentially significant to you as an applicant!:

Reputation and Mission

- Outstanding P.S. [Public School] district.
- Committed to excellence.
- Focusing on diversity.
- An 80-year-old college preparatory school that stresses academic excellence for its 400 students in Grades K–12.
- Nationally acclaimed suburban school district.
- If you believe in the right of all students to succeed, we appeal to you to consider joining our winning team.
- Progressive K–8 school district.
- Prominent independent school enrolling 700 pre-K–Grade 12 students.
- Visit us on our Web site: www......

Benefits

- Competitive salaries.
- Generous compensation and benefits package.
- After-school [paid positions] available.
- Salary based on experience and credentials.

Responsiveness to Diversity

- Minority candidates encouraged to apply.
- We are proud to be an equal opportunity employer, pursuing diversity and the value it brings to the workplace.
- AA (Affirmative Action).
- EOE (Equal Opportunity Employer).
- M/F (male or female).

Whereas some ads highlight qualities of the educational programs, the reputation of the school or district, and the academic culture, others focus on the financial remunerations available or the desire to be an inclusive community. The absence or presence of these comments may cause you to make inferences about the school's priorities that will contribute to your deliberations about which districts you choose to consider.

Take the time now to circle your tentative choices from the range of school characteristics we discussed. Use the empty column in Table 2.5 to note the additional characteristics that are important to you.

SCHOOL PREFERENCES

You should be aware that schools and districts have preferences as well. Some qualifications that have appeared in newspaper advertisements include these:

Experience

- Qualified and experienced educators.
- Thematic, integrated teaching experience preferred.
- Applicants for all positions are expected to be computer literate.

Certification

- State certification.
- Additional special education certification and/or certification in reading preferred.
- Dual certification preferred (generally suggests special education, bilingual education, reading/literacy, or early childhood along with elementary or a secondary subject area).

Academic Degrees

- M.A. (Master of Arts degree).
- M.A. in ECE (Master of Arts degree with a concentration in early childhood education).

Expect that districts will require documentation of your certification, academic degree(s), and experiences. This may involve making a photocopy of your official certification, obtaining official transcripts from your college, or seeking a letter from the principal of the school in which you taught.

The identified preferences (in contrast to requirements) are not absolutes. Districts indicate that they prefer to employ teachers with these characteristics. In the instances where they indicate "only," it would probably be foolish to apply unless you meet the qualifications. When the term *preferred* is used, you are certainly free to apply, but do not be surprised if there is no follow-up.

The advertisements and listings offer a brief description of what the school district identifies as the most important issues in selecting its candidates. Some terms are intended to be suggestive of a larger issue. For example, M.A. indicates a preference for

Table 2.5 My Tentative Choices

ISSUES	Geography	Funding	Length & Type	Title	Assignment	Grade(s)	Specialization(s)	School Characteristics
CHOICES	Local	Public	Anticipated vacancy	Teacher	Full-time	Pre-K	Generalist	
	Relocate	Private/independent	Leave replacement	Assistant teacher	Part-time	K–4	Content specialist	
		Combined private and public	Immediate opening	Substitute teacher	Long-term substitute	Middle school	Interdisciplinary	
			Tenure-track		Per diem substitute	High school	Reading/literacy	
							Family & careers	
							Gifted	
							Special education	

NOTES NOTES NOTES

candidates with a generic master's degree, not necessarily restricted to candidates who graduated from programs with a Master of Arts degree. Thus, a person with an M.S. degree in education may be equally attractive to the district. A notation of M.A. in ECE is intended to suggest the need for an early childhood education specialization on the graduate level, which might result in a degree labeled M.A., M.S., or M.S. in education.

You are responsible for interpreting these descriptions and honestly presenting your experiences in such a way that your background is attractive to the districts where you want your application considered. When there are terms that are new to you, ask other educational professionals to help you interpret them, or you might contact the school district to clarify your understanding. In your communication with the school, make sure that you are perceived as a serious and capable professional.

In addition to all the explicit criteria established in job searches, there are frequently unwritten, subjective practices as well. For example, residents may get preference over outsiders. Current employees, either substitutes or teacher assistants, may be given priority. Relatives of high-ranking officials may circumvent many steps in the process.

There are many unpredictable events influencing who gets a given position. If there is an immediate need, the search is limited. If there is time, there is likely to be an extended search and therefore more competition.

Searching for a position is rife with tension. If you present yourself well and maintain an optimistic perspective, you will eventually find a position that will nurture your continued professional and personal development.

Recognizing the unique qualities of each school setting, you will envision the specific activities and characteristics that are essential or nonnegotiable for you and those that might be nice, but are not of great consequence. The fewer nonnegotiable factors you identify, the more choices you will have. If you limit the number of places where you apply, you will be able to truly explore each one in depth. You will be able to utilize this increased knowledge of the school in responding to questions at your interview. However, if you restrict yourself to too few settings, you may find yourself without a position! Only you can decide the right number of places to pursue.

To make your decisions, you may start with the decision trees, circling the places where you would prefer to work. An alternative strategy is to choose from the posted listings and advertisements. A third strategy is to identify schools with philosophies similar to your own, based on your experiences and on advice given to you by colleagues, professors, cooperating teachers, and mentors, and from your familiarity with current literature on schools.

NOTES NOTES NOTES

You need not limit yourself to those schools that have advertised. Take it as your responsibility to find schools where you want to teach. Inquire about available positions. Often your presence in the school building is the surest way to get an interview. Be proactive and persistent.

SUMMING UP

There is probably no such thing as a perfect job. Your success as a new teacher is certainly enhanced by finding the ideal match with a school's preferences. Finding your teaching placement will require you to either shape the opportunity into the most perfect job it can be for you or to continue to look for a better fit. You may duplicate Table 2.5 to help you as you consider your many choices.

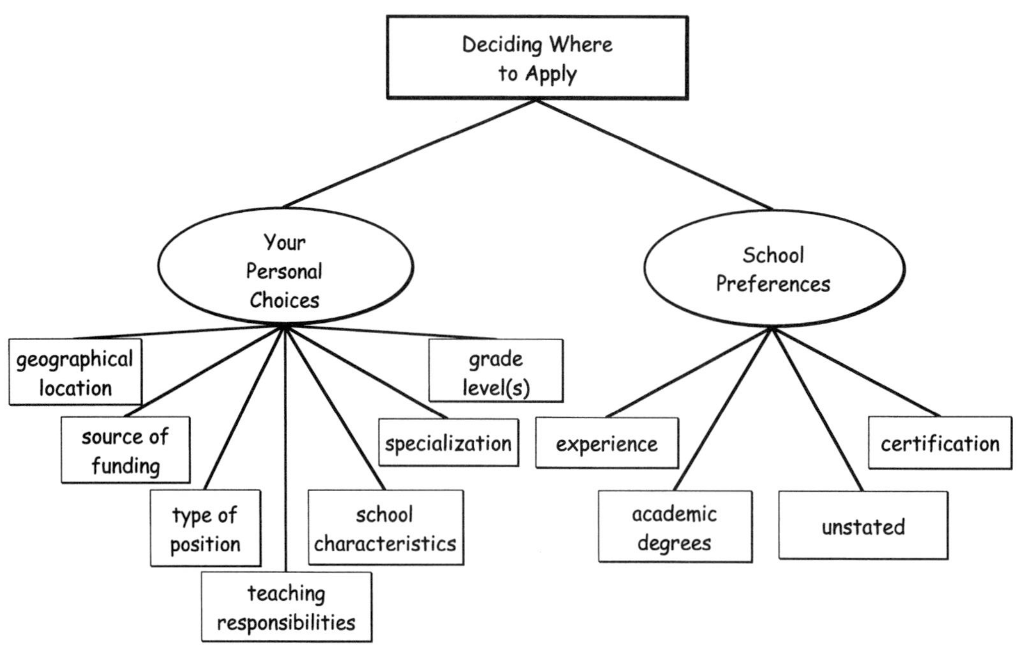

Remember that to be a teacher you need to be hired for a teaching position! If you really want to teach, you will find a good position. Just keep on looking.

SUPPLEMENTARY RESOURCES

United States

- American Association for Employment in Education
  820 Davis Street, Suite 222
  Evanston, IL 60201-1999
  847/864-1999

- National Association of Independent Schools
  1620 L Street, NW
  Washington, DC 20036

- Recruiting New Teachers Inc.
  385 Concord Avenue, Suite 100
  Belmont, MA
  617/489-6000

- United States Departments of Education
  http://ericps.ed.uiuc.edu/eece/statlink.html

International

- *Assignment Overseas: A Planning Guide*
  IRC for Curriculum and Materials Exchange
  P.O. Box 020470
  Tuscaloosa, AL 35402

- Fulbright Teacher Exchange
  U.S. Information Agency
  301 Fourth Street, SW
  Washington, DC 20547

- *The International Educator*
  P.O. Box 513-A
  Cummaquid, MA 02637

- U.S. Department of Defense Schools
  Recruitment Section
  4040 North Fairfax Drive, Sixth Floor
  Arlington, VA 22203

- U.S. Department of State
  Office of Overseas Schools
  Room 245, SA29 A/OS
  Washington, DC 20522

- University of Northern Iowa
  Overseas Placement Service for Educators
  Cedar Falls, IA 50614

PART B

GETTING READY TO APPLY

Now that you have narrowed your choices and gathered some information about schools, you are ready to organize the documents that will introduce you as a candidate. A successful job search requires you to obtain and update information about potential openings and to track the progress of each of your applications. As Jennifer interviews with several professionals at Public School 33, she takes the opportunity to elaborate on many activities listed in her application documents. You will see how to set the stage in preparation for an interview.

In Chapter 3, Organizing the Application Process, we offer suggestions and samples of ways to stay organized. Typically, your cover letter and résumé introduce your candidacy to a school. You want these to make a positive first impression that will lead to an interview. Chapter 4, Assembling Your Application Documents, guides the development of the required and supplementary documents that enhance your application.

Scenario:	Jennifer Eddy An Initial Interview With a School-Based Team
Chapter 3	Organizing the Application Process
Chapter 4	Assembling Your Application Documents

SCENARIO

JENNIFER EDDY

An Initial Interview With a School-Based Team

Candidate:	Jennifer Eddy	
Interviewers:	Evelyn Hill	Principal
	Annette Furillo	Assistant Principal
	Jan Pell	School Psychologist
	Marie Tescher	Teacher

Jennifer's interview is school-based involving a four-member team (the principal, Evelyn Hill; an assistant principal in charge of special education, Annette Furillo; the school psychologist, Jan Pell; and a fourth-grade teacher who is also the union chairperson, Marie Tescher). The team at P.S. 33 has worked together for several years. They fill openings in the staff by "paper screening" multiple résumés and agreeing on those few who will be called for an interview. Jennifer Eddy is here for her first interview at the school. As you read the scenario consider the information Jennifer conveys in her responses and how you might answer the very same questions. We offer focused questions coupled with our interpretations of the ongoing interview.

WHO IS JENNIFER?

Jennifer is a city person, born and bred. She attended a university in the city, scorning the idea of going away when her parents suggested it. She knows the city inside and out, the people, the places, and now its children, as she student taught in city schools. She's comfortable in this setting and jokes about the purity of air and landscapes she experiences when visiting friends and relatives in the suburbs. She claims the "burbs are a nice place to visit." One can appreciate Jennifer's sense of humor on first meeting her. She loves the city and is particularly entranced with the diversity of cultures and ethnic groups. It is no wonder that she is determined to find a teaching position in the city.

HOW DID SHE GET AN INTERVIEW?

Jennifer examined the telephone directory, noting the names of 20 schools accessible by train from her home. She called each for the spelling of the principal's name so she could send her résumé and cover letter to a specific person. She's heard from five schools and has been invited for interviews at two. "Not bad for a first attempt," she believed. Jennifer is convinced that she wants to make a difference in the lives of these children, and so she welcomes this interview as a major step in the process. She can hardly contain her excitement as Ms. Hill, the principal, introduced the people around the table.

THE INTERVIEW

Ms. Hill: We would like you to tell us a little about yourself and why you would like to teach at P.S. 33. We'll ask you some specific questions and leave time for you to ask questions of us. Why don't you start by telling us something about yourself?

Jennifer: I am completing an intensive teacher preparation course at ____________ University here in the city, and I feel terribly knowledgeable about the field of education because of my courses and experiences in schools. Not only did I learn the content that K–6 students will be learning, but I also learned about myself. We kept reflective journals which asked us to look inward to see ourselves as teachers and learners. I feel I am well on the way to understanding children, learning, and teaching.

Ms. Furillo: That's interesting. Can you tell us more?

Jennifer: The students in my student teaching experience were economically poor and from diverse cultures. One of my jobs was to customize the curriculum through individual learning plans

NOTES NOTES NOTES

for three fourth-grade children who spoke little English. I learned a great deal about how children learn from that experience.

I had the opportunity to use my interest in photography to work with parents and local businesspeople in a partnership. The children compiled biographical sketches of people in a senior citizen residence as a basis for understanding the history of the neighborhood. They took photos to document their observations and their stories. They loved that project and so did I. The students and I got to know more about the community, and our neighbors got to know more about us and our school. The PTA helped us create a book and we displayed it at the annual block party. I have a copy of it in my portfolio if you would like to see it. [1]

How did Jennifer help her interviewers get to know her better?

Ms. Furillo: That sounds very exciting, Jennifer. Can you tell us how you accommodated those who had difficulty writing?

Jennifer: Yes. I worked with struggling writers individually for 2 or 3 months building on their interests before we got into the Senior Citizen Interview Project. By the time we were to begin the project, all the students were doing some writing. In one case, Johnny tape-recorded his story and asked Jimmy to transcribe it. As it turned out, Jimmy and Johnny decided to work as partners.

Ms. Furillo: How did you prepare the class for the actual interviewing?

Jennifer: We listed potential questions to focus our interviews. The students placed these on clipboards as they prepared for their interviews. One student was very concerned about using only words she knew were correctly spelled. This limited her fluency, but we were able to get her to go beyond that by putting her on the class computer. Using spell check relieved her tension about misspelled words.

What other activities would you have offered for English language learners?

Ms. Furillo: What did you do about those English language learners you spoke about?

KEEP IN MIND

[1]Jennifer was expansive in the information she provided the interviewers about herself: her university preparation in curriculum and teaching, her philosophy about hands-on learning, and her relationship with the community. She showed how she used her hobby as a way to excite her students in the classroom. In customizing curriculum for English language learners she demonstrated her ability to identify learning needs and to develop curriculum around these needs. She focused on experiences and talents that would benefit her students and omitted extraneous personal information.

Jennifer: In a small group we illustrated, labeled, and read the stories we created. They shared these with the rest of the class. They were writing and becoming more confident with English. By November 1st, they were all ready to participate in the Senior Citizen Interview Project even though they were at different levels of readiness. [2]

How would you respond to Ms. Tescher's question?

Ms. Tescher: What do you think your students learned from this project and how do you know what they have learned?

Jennifer: How do I know what my students learned from the project? Well, when I plan a unit such as the Senior Citizen Interview Project, I ask myself, "What do I want them to learn?" I build in evaluations, benchmarks for me and for the children. In our teacher preparation program we were introduced to Tyler's four curriculum questions:

1. What will you teach?

2. To whom will you teach it?

3. How will you teach it?

4. How will you know you were successful?

I even add a fifth dimension of my own. I ask, "Why is it important to learn this information?" Built into this curriculum plan is an automatic assessment to help me see what they're learning. [3]

Ms. Tescher: You say you saw what they were learning. Was there any way the students could identify what they learned from the project?

Jennifer: I put in a couple of questions to help the students to see how successful they were. They might end the project saying, "Okay, I learned how to map out a series of interview questions and I was able to put the list onto the computer. But I

KEEP IN MIND

[2]Jennifer is "listening" to the questions. She described how she helped children in small groups and individually. She built on student interest and related the methods she used to enhance learning. Jennifer conveyed a somewhat superficial understanding of the writing process. She might want to consider developing a more comprehensive discussion of writing in the classroom for subsequent interviews.

[3]Jennifer repeated the question. The interviewer can always correct it at this point if he or she meant the conversation to go in another direction. This repetition gave Jennifer a little more time to organize her response. *(continued)*

went off on a tangent. Next time I'll stick to my questions." Another question they addressed is, "What is one thing you learned that you could teach to a classmate?" One student wrote, "I learned about using quotation marks for nicknames. I knew about using quotation marks for something someone said, but not for other things like nicknames." This kind of information became a strategy that I could add to the next mini-grammar lesson I would teach.

NOTES NOTES NOTES

Ms. Hill: Jennifer, we have many people applying for this position of fourth-grade teacher; tell us why we should hire you.

How would you respond to Ms. Hill's request, "Tell us why we should hire you"?

Jennifer: Well, I'll be a strong teacher in this school. I've wanted to be a teacher for a long time and I've been looking forward to my first day. My student teaching experience helped me to know I made the right decision. I learned so much right along with the children. I really love it when I see children trying to master a particular skill.

Ms. Tescher: Tell us about a successful lesson you have taught.

Jennifer: When I was student teaching in kindergarten my cooperating teacher's reading program was very full with literature. I prepared a lesson incorporating a read aloud, discussion, and writing. We had been talking about family members, and helping, and caring so I chose a book called *A Chair For My Mother* [Williams, 1982]. We gathered on the rug and talked for a while about all the work moms and dads do. I read the book and we had a wonderful discussion about all the events in the book. When the discussion ended I asked the children what they'd like to "write" about. They began writing stories and drawing pictures. I love it when I overhear students cooperating on spelling a particular word, especially if these little ones are kindergarten children having a very serious discussion on whether or not the word *chair* starts with *tc* or *ch*. [4]

KEEP IN MIND

Jennifer responded to the second part of the question, "How do you know what your students have learned?" She stressed several educational beliefs: Children can take responsibility for their learning, children can learn to do self-assessment, and assessment is an ongoing process.

She didn't offer specific examples of ways to evaluate student performance, and Ms. Tescher was clearly trying to find out how Jennifer evaluates what students have learned. Concrete examples, using Tyler's four curriculum questions, and the fifth one that Jennifer added would enhance her response significantly.

[4]Jennifer is knowledgeable about some reading and writing strategies. She went so far as to relate an entire lesson for kindergartners mentioning reading, writing, and phonics. She made sure her interviewers were aware that she considers reading a purposeful learning activity.

NOTES NOTES NOTES

Ms. Tescher: Can you describe the classroom you might create if we hired you? What would it look like?

Jennifer: My classroom will have a great library. I have been collecting award winners since my first reading course at the university. We'll have a large collection of books with diverse cultures to help us know about each other's roots. We'll have lots of good picture books. I was successful when I student taught in sixth grade and read picture books like *Jumanji* and *Polar Express* by Chris Van Allsburg.

Our literacy program will focus on good literature, writing, and phonics to put my students on the path to becoming lifelong lovers of reading and writing. I'll have a writing center and a listening center with a number of tapes to go along with books in my classroom library. Then all I'll need is a jack and four headphones and my listening center is up and running. We'll have multiple copies of these books so each child can listen to the tape and follow along with her or his own book. And the writing center will have tons of different kinds of paper and writing tools. [5]

Ms. Furillo: Jennifer, we all know there are good days and bad days in life. Can you share with us your worst day in student teaching?

Jennifer: I don't love talking about it, but I do look upon it as a learning experience. My field coordinator asked me to conduct a math lesson for the second-grade class. I knew that they were learning fractions and I knew that they had discussed whole and half. I designed a lesson dealing mainly with quarters. We planned to use the manipulatives in the classroom and fake money from the math center.

So we gathered on the rug. They weren't listening and I kept saying louder and louder, "Excuse me! Children! Please!" Finally I got them all on the rug except one boy. I called his name so many times that some children began chanting, "Joel, Joel,"

KEEP IN MIND

[5]Jennifer provided a picture of a classroom with many learning centers. She considers learning as purposeful and would be sensitive to the needs of all children as she stocks her library. When describing the listening center she showed she was aware of the preliminary preparation needed. We get a clear understanding of Jennifer's classroom as it reflects her plans for reading instruction. She might consider giving equal time to a discussion of math, science, and social studies instruction so her interviewers may see that indeed she will be a teacher of all subjects.

over and over. I could see the other children getting impatient so I left the group on the rug and dragged Joel gently into the circle. He was noisy and this upset the rest of the group—hardly a good learning environment. I was tempted to ask my cooperating teacher for help, but we agreed we'd make this lesson as "real" as possible. She would assist only in an emergency.

NOTES NOTES NOTES

The children were responsive but anxious to get to the manipulatives they saw in the center of the rug. I spent a great deal of time insisting that they wait until I showed them the "whole" broken into the "half," which I would then break into "quarters." I really spent a lot of time planning and I wanted to go through my agenda as planned. Looking back, it seems that it could have been a very different lesson. I learned a great deal that day. It certainly was an eye opener.

Dr. Pell: If you could do the lesson again, how would you do it differently? What have you learned?

Jennifer: What did I learn? Well I learned a lot about three important classroom issues: organization, materials, and discipline.

First, organization: I think I expected the students to listen to me the way they listened to my cooperating teacher, and now I know I have to earn that. In my class I will start building listening skills on Day 1. We'll practice coming to the rug as a group during the early part of the year. Even if it takes weeks we will practice. Classroom organization doesn't just happen. I know that now.

Second, manipulatives: I know now that any kind of materials have to be allotted beforehand. They can be put into individual envelopes for each child or at a central spot for the "collector" to get and bring back to the group. Again I learned the hard way.

Third, discipline: When Joel was getting upset initially, I should have dealt with him individually before he started to upset the whole group. Behavior is contagious. I think now nipping it in the bud, if possible, is a better approach. I might have used him as my special helper. I might have taken his hand and walked to the rug as the others were gathering. I might have gotten him a buddy.

What did you learn from Jennifer's description of her "worst day" experience?

I have learned that there is more than one kind of planning. There's planning for the concepts the children are learning and there's the planning for the logistical side of learning.

This planning then becomes much more comprehensive. I learned some important lessons that day. [6]

Ms. Hill: Jennifer, thank you so much for coming in and helping us to get to know you. As we told you, we have many applicants for this position and we have many interviews to conduct before we make our decisions. But we will be in touch with you just as soon as we know. It was very nice meeting you.

KEEP IN MIND

[6]We have all had "worst days" in our careers. Jennifer did some things that might invite criticism, such as gently dragging Joel to the rug and raising her voice to gain control, but she learned some important lessons. She learned that anticipating disruption might prevent it. Dealing with misbehaving children is always a challenge, and Jennifer called on some strategies she will add to as she goes along in her career. She learned some aspects for organizing a lesson and distributing materials. Jennifer seemed to focus on elements of the curriculum without really having a comprehensive sense of larger issues. She might consider other ways to organize for large-group instruction and add strategies for small-group instruction to her repertoire.

SUMMING UP

Jennifer conveyed a strong sense of self by talking about her hobby and how she will use it in the classroom. Having practiced responding to potential questions, she presented an astute analysis of positive and negative experiences. She communicated her beliefs, while displaying her knowledge sincerely. She was confident, humorous, and analytical about her mistakes. She was resourceful and eager to learn. These are laudable attributes, evident when we listen to Jennifer. She is a teacher:

T — Tireless in her efforts
E — Enthusiastic in her approach
A — Analytical about her mistakes
C — Confident in herself
H — Honest and humorous
E — Eager to learn
R — Resourceful

CHAPTER 3 ORGANIZING THE APPLICATION PROCESS

AT A GLANCE

This chapter offers suggestions for the organization and maintenance of the information you gather in your job search. We address:

- Organizing your information.
- Formatting your application system.

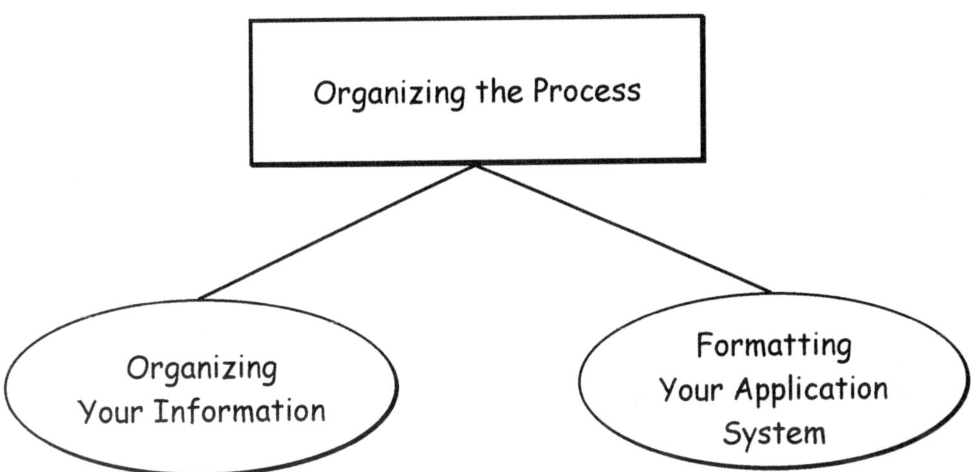

Beginning the complex task of applying for a teaching position can be stressful to those who are new to this task. Let's look at some snapshots of new candidates as they begin.

SNAPSHOT 1

My cooperating teacher gave me a note indicating that there are two leave replacement openings in her friend's district. An announcement of one opening in my cooperating district was posted on the office bulletin board, and I made a photocopy of it. And the ads! There were three ads this weekend for positions in districts near me!

I have to get more information from my cooperating teacher about her friend's school. Who shall I talk to about the opening in my district? And now I have a collection of snips of newspaper ads. Where do I put them? How can I keep these pieces of paper organized?

SNAPSHOT 2

Finally! A positive letter from a school district. They're interested in me and they're requesting that I call for an appointment to be interviewed. Great! I sent out personalized cover letters and résumés to 20 different districts, and I am getting an interview. I am so ready!

Wait a moment! Is that the school district that advertised for kindergarten teachers or is it the one that emphasized dual certification? Where is the cover letter I sent to that district? I have my general cover letter, but I know I changed it a bit for this district. Where is it now? And the résumé! What did I emphasize? Did I provide more detail about kindergarten or was it the planning for the special-needs children that I emphasized? What will I say?

Will these be your questions? Will *you* be ready? Can you easily access and review your materials? Or will you spend so much time locating the necessary materials that you have no time to prepare for the interview? How can you avoid this predicament?

A successful job search requires organization. You will be gathering much information from many sources—your teacher education courses, your field work experiences, and many conversations with educators and friends. The usefulness of your information depends on how complete it is and on how easily you may retrieve material when you need it. As a teacher candidate, you want not only to appear organized, but to be organized. Therefore, it is essential to develop a reliable system to store many types of information and retrieve specific information about each of your applications. This will help you manage the multiple steps in your application process in a prompt and professional way.

NOTES NOTES NOTES

ORGANIZING YOUR INFORMATION

The multiple types of information you gather in your job search may be organized in many different ways. We suggest the following three overlapping components (see Fig. 3.1).

1. **Application file** The main file containing all the information you gather about the position plus all your communications with the school.

2. **Action abstract** A composite "to do" list of your application status.

3. **Professional networking address book** Contacts in education.

ACTION ABSTRACT

File ID	School/District	Deadline	Date Sent	Ackn. Rec'd	Response	Follow-up
1	Ocean Ave.Elem Hillsboro S.D.	Unsolicited -cold inquiry	4/12	4/30	No Openings	Not Active
2	Ellensville S.D.	7/1	6/20	6/28	Req. for Interview 7/12	

FIG. 3.1. Components of a sample application system.

The *application file* is the repository for all the information you acquire about each potential opening—from the first casual comment made by a cooperating teacher to your notes following

NOTES NOTES NOTES

your interview with the superintendent. Each application you submit warrants an individual file in which you record all the information you have about the position and the school. It should also include notations on each contact you have made, as well as all the dates pertinent to that application.

The range of information that an application file might contain is extensive and is detailed in Table 3.1.

Successful preparation for your interviews and for your multiple contacts with the school will depend on the accuracy and comprehensiveness of the information you record. Figure 3.2 is a sample of a notebook-style application file. You should immediately enter each piece of information as you become aware of it.

In addition to organizing your application files you may create an *action abstract*, or overview table, summarizing the status of each application. Because each application may continue to grow as long as it is active, quick access is very helpful. The action abstract allows you to assess at a glance which contacts are due for a follow-up call or letter and which ones sent a negative response, and therefore should be removed from your current concerns. The action abstract may include only enough information to keep track of the actions taken or to be taken, as listed in Table 3.2.

Table 3.1 Information in an Application File

- School/district name
- Type of position:
  - Grade level
  - School
  - Responsibilities
  - Number of positions
- Source of information:
  - Advertisement (copy from newspaper)
  - Personal contact
- Date of information
- Date application is due
- Materials sent to school:
  - Copies of:
    - Cover letter
    - Résumé
    - Application
    - Credential File
    - Reference letters
- Date mailed
- Contacts from school:
  - Acknowledgment of receipt of your application
  - Positive follow-up
    - Schedule for an interview
    - Schedule for a writing sample
    - Schedule for a demonstration lesson
  - Negative response
- Actions for you to take:
  - Follow-up visits
  - Letters
  - Phone calls
- Phone contacts:
  - Name, date, direct phone number
- School information:
  - Neighborhood characteristics
  - Curriculum focus
  - Size
  - Organization of school

NOTES NOTES NOTES

Application DUE - July 1
Sent - June 20

Ellensville S.D.

Ad – Daily Record June 3
3 elem. Positions
5 schools – 3 elem. (North, Cross Ave., Jackson)
1 Jr. HS, 1 HS
Reading Recovery used in Cross Ave.

Coop teacher – Mrs. Ellis – has children in Cross Ave. School

Acknowledgment Received – June 28
Signed by J.D. Clark
Director of Personnel

Request for Interview rec. – July 12
Signed by Ms. Mary Downs,
Principal, North Elem.

FIG. 3.2. Sample application file entry.

A clear organizational table, such as in Fig. 3.3, is a quick overview of the actions associated with each application. It can be easily updated causing "to do" items to stand out.

You will benefit from developing a *professional networking address book* to contain the names of people you contact during the application process. When you have acquired a teaching position, your application files will be stored away, but those professional contacts can be a benefit throughout your career. To prevent losing names and phone numbers, gather the contact information from your application file in a separate and permanent professional networking address book. Supplement it with other contacts such as professors, cooperating teachers, and others who are knowledgeable about education and schools.

Table 3.2 Information in the Action Abstract

- Location of full record (page number or file name)
- School or district name
- Application due date
- Date of acknowledgment
- School or district response
- Follow-ups

File ID	School / District	Deadline	Date Sent	Acknowledgment Received	Response: Positive or Negative	Follow-up
1	Ocean Ave.Elem Hillsboro S.D.	Unsolicited – cold inquiry	4/12	4/30	No Openings	Not Active
2	Ellensville S.D.	7/1	6/20	6/28	Request for Interview - 7/12	
3	Hampton S.D.	7/20	7/12	7/25	Appt. for Writing Sample 8/10	
				8/17	Interview 8/22	Thank you 8/23

FIG. 3.3. Sample action abstract.

You will meet many of the same people at professional conferences and school meetings, and you should sustain good relationships with colleagues in the relatively small world of educators. Your professional networking address book may help your memory at crucial times. Table 3.3 lists the categories of information that can be useful in this book.

A small binder is one appropriate form for your professional networking address book. It is flexible, portable, and easily updated. An index card file is another good choice. It has flexible space and is expandable, but may not be convenient to carry with you. Electronic organizers certainly can be useful, especially with their capability for searching by categories (name, title, or school). If you use an electronic database, you may create separate searchable fields for each category of information. A sample paper page containing updated information may look like Fig. 3.4. Jane Siegel and Mr. Green represent fieldwork cooperating teachers with whom you may wish to stay in contact. You might ask Dr. Simon, now department chair in your teacher education college, to recommend you for a position. Cross-referencing your contacts by entering each one under the person's name and under the school or institution name provides options for greater recall in the future.

Table 3.3 Information in a Professional Networking Address Book

- Name, address, phone, e-mail, fax (home, school)
- Title, position, responsibilities
- Event where met
- School affiliation
- Date of contact

Jane Siegel	Northwood Elementary School Works with Ms. Susan Trost	Spring 2001
36 First Lane Spring Valley, NY	Tyndel Lane Crestwood, NY	1st Grade Cooperating Teacher
914-xxx-xxxx e-mail:	914-xxx-xxxx	
o		
Dr. Mark Simon	Maryhill College Reading Professor	Fall 2000
361-xxx-xxxx A+ **6/9/01 became Dept. Chair**	Worked on integrated project in Rison Elem. School –	
Phyllis Sims	neighbor, teaches in Smith St. School	April 2001
704-xxx-xxx	thinks there will be two openings	
o		S
Schefferson School Murther Place, Hillsboro, IN	Field Exp. 6th grade Literacy Program Ms. Mary O'Connor, Princ. Mr. Green- 6th grade Coop. Teacher	Fall '99
132-xxx-xxxx		
o		
Bob Snyder Capwell School	Newspapers in Education Workshop 4th grade teacher, ***lots of retirements soon*** ***	6/99
Birchville, ID 345-xxx-xxxx		

FIG. 3.4. Sample networking address page.

This brief overview suggests the types of information you might gather as you create an organized database for your job search and for your teaching career. Let's now consider how you might format a file system that is functional and efficient.

FORMATTING YOUR APPLICATION SYSTEM

Taking time to conceptualize and develop your personal application system will save you much time and stress when you are under pressure to prepare for interviews. Customize your own format so you don't end up with important information scattered on scraps of paper. Your format should reflect how you like to work and what you're comfortable with. Consider your style of working:

- Are you a filer? Have you previously developed a reliable and efficient filing system for your professional materials? Then you might be comfortable formatting your application system as a series of paper file folders within your current file cabinet.

• Are you chronologically oriented? If so, you may use a notebook that you can divide into sections for each application and enter each application chronologically.

• Are you comfortable with computers and with computerized files, folders, and directories? If so, you may wish to create an electronic file for the materials you generate. You may even be able to scan each advertisement and store each electronically, creating a paperless file.

You need to choose the format that is most convenient for you to maintain. Consider the following formats:

- File folders.
- Book file.
- Electronic file.

A traditional file folder system can be used for your application file. A separate folder for each application allows you to insert documents as you receive them. Some candidates have found pocket or prong folders useful. The action abstract can be easily accessed in a separate file folder in front of all the other files. You may even choose a different color for this folder.

For organizing an application file, some candidates create a book file that is self-contained and easily reviewed and updated. If you choose a bound or spiral book, dedicate at least four pages for each application record. Reserve a separate section for the expanding action abstract and clearly mark it with tabs for easy access.

A looseleaf binder has great flexibility: It can be expanded as the need arises, and it offers the advantage of having optional "pocket" pages into which you can insert letters from the school.

The typical organization in a book file is chronological. You create the record of the application as soon as you see the ad, hear about the teaching position, or identify a school of interest to you. All other information is inserted on a daily basis.

NOTES NOTES NOTES

An electronic file can be very efficient for those who are comfortable with organizing folders or directories on a computer. The cover letter and the résumé you create on a computer can be easily modified for subsequent applications. You can save the modified version using the school name as part of the filename. Such computer files are very easy to retrieve (and save much paper).

You can maintain your action abstract on your computer using either a tables function or a spreadsheet program. Be sure to clearly identify the action abstract by using a distinctive name. Using the numeral 1 before the filename will assure that it is listed before all the files that start with the customary alphabet characters. The information in the action abstract can be updated easily and printed when necessary. If a spreadsheet is used, the records can be reorganized as the need presents itself. For instance, if you have received three letters of rejection, you might want to put those records at the end of your directory because they are no longer active and will be retained only for a future job search. In the sample action abstract (Fig. 3.3), the Ocean Avenue Elementary School record can be moved to the bottom of the list because it is not active at this time. The Ellensville and Hampton school districts' applications are still open and active.

A computerized file may be cross-referenced to a paper file containing acknowledgments and other responses. The information you gather as you research a district can also be stored in the paper file with a notation in your computer record. Scanning documents into your computer would enable you to store each application's complete record in digitized form. Carefully name each file to facilitate finding it. Do not hesitate to rename your files as you find more efficient ways to organize your growing database.

A security factor exists with computers. Routine backup copies of your job search folder should be made on external diskettes or other backup systems to avoid loss of your documents. If you develop a computer problem and find that your files are not accessible, you will be devastated. Frequent backups can spare you great frustration. Some people keep parallel files in print form as a security measure.

SUMMING UP

Having easy access to all the information you so carefully gathered about each potential position will contribute to your thorough preparation for a successful interview. You should review your information about the position (the original advertisement, announcement, or contact person), your research about the school and neighborhood, and your coordinating application documents as necessary preparation for an interview. A carefully organized and personalized application system will be a major asset in your job search.

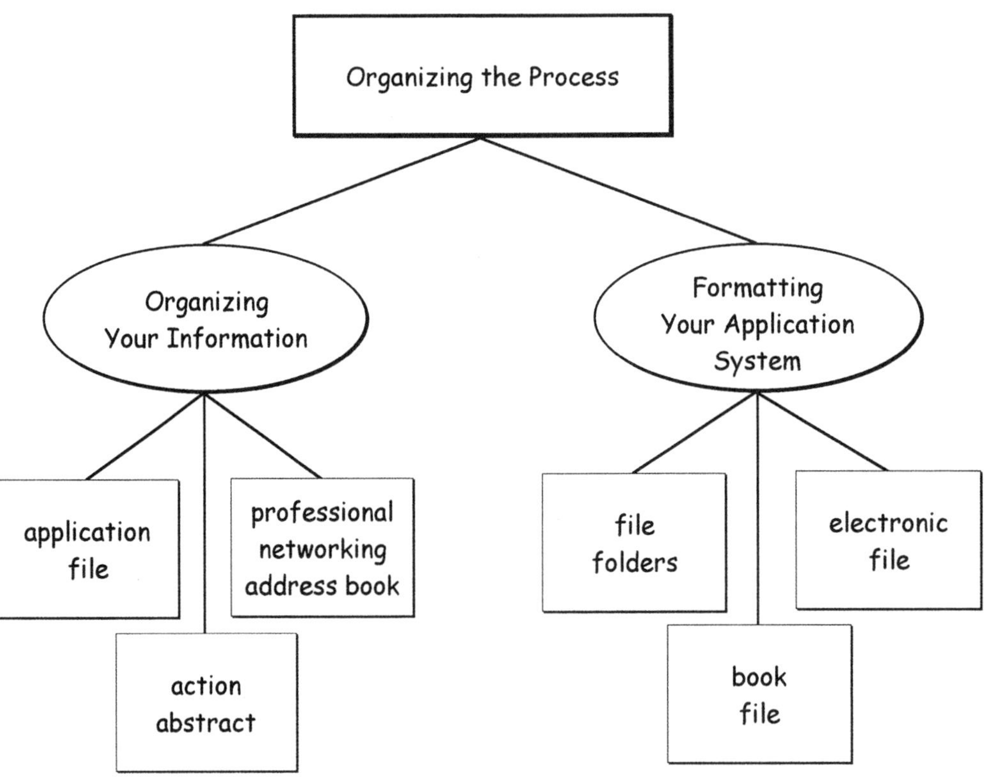

CHAPTER 4

ASSEMBLING YOUR APPLICATION DOCUMENTS

AT A GLANCE

We will consider the documents you will use when applying for a teaching position. You will create some and you will gather others from diverse sources.

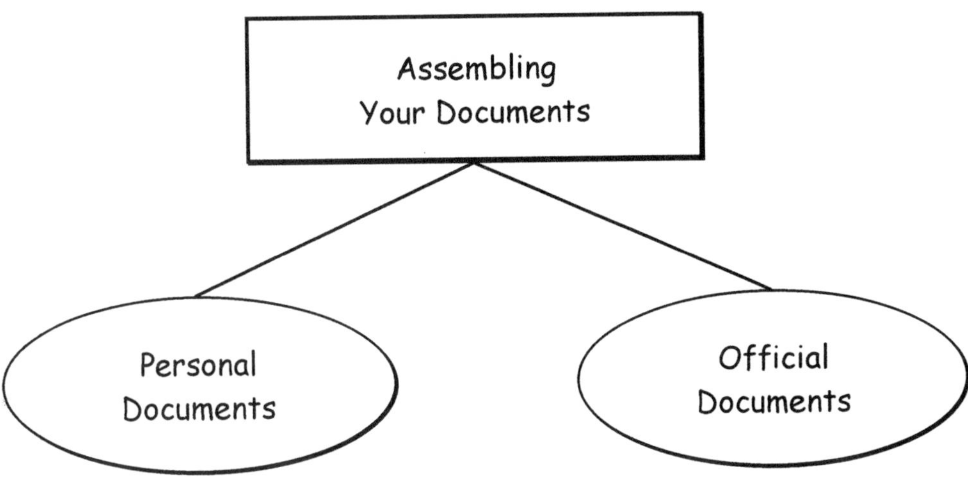

You introduce your name and qualifications with the documents you present to a school during the application process. These documents usually include a cover letter, a résumé, letters of recommendation, an application form, official documents, and a professional credential file. Although all of these documents represent you, you do not have complete control over their form and content. Some of them you will create; others are issued to you; still others are created by those you have asked to support your candidacy.

PERSONAL DOCUMENTS

You will create cover letters and résumés and you want them to be unique in communicating your professionalism, your style, and your special characteristics and how they connect with each school. Make your materials easy to read, clear in thought, and filled with information that is appealing to potential employers. Be sure that your documents are impressive and effective on their own because you will have no chance to interpret the information for the reader. Consider these five guiding principles in preparing your documents:

1. *Communicate your unique qualities.* Focus on three aspects of this process. Identify events and activities that influenced your growth as a person and as an educator. Analyze each experience for its connection to a classroom situation. Create an accurate reflection of your personality and background.

2. *Customize each application.* You will want to appeal to the broadest possible audience while being true to your carefully considered values. You may wonder about your audience. You might ask: Is the reader an education "traditionalist"? Is the reader an advocate of creativity in teaching? Recognize each school's uniqueness. It is important to carefully read the position announcement, analyze the information you have researched on the school, and adjust your documents to emphasize the match between you and the school.

3. *Brag about your accomplishments.* The school wants information about your skills, experiences, and successes. Don't make them guess! Express who you are and what you can bring to the position without overstating the case. One candidate who organized and supervised a busy office neglected to mention this on her résumé, believing that activities outside of education would not be valued. On the other hand, one candidate aggrandized a babysitting experience into a "preschool teaching experience," which was untruthful and unwise. Be cautious about overstating (or understating) your achievements.

4. *Be accurate.* A seemingly trivial spelling mistake can cause your application to be removed from further review. When documenting your experiences, verify the accuracy of dates and names to establish the credibility of your application. Have your documents read by several people including someone who is not an educator. Find a good proofreader. Consider all suggestions.

5. *Make documents e-mail ready.* Increasing numbers of schools have Web sites and are communicating electronically. Schools may advertise on the Internet, especially when there is an urgent need to fill a position. They may request or prefer your application by fax or e-mail. When submitting materials electronically, evaluate the formatting you use (fonts, graphics, tables) because some formats may disappear, become distorted, or transmit poorly. Take whatever time is necessary to verify that each document is accurate and complete prior to sending it. You may wish to send an additional copy of your materials by surface mail to ensure their receipt in good form.

As you search for a teaching position, your cover letter and résumé are your primary documents. We offer some general guidance here, knowing you will also find great detail about these initial documents elsewhere. You want your materials to be selected from the many applications a school receives and placed on the short list of people to be interviewed.

A cover letter serves as a bridge between the job posting and your résumé. It introduces you, informs the reader why you are forwarding your résumé, and identifies the position for which you want to be considered. It is a powerful, formal, one-page document that determines whether the reader will even turn to your résumé. Remember that the first person to see application letters may be a secretary who will catalog and sort them. Use a subject line or the first sentence to indicate the position you are seeking. Customize your cover letter to promote your match for this school. Use the name of the school in the body of the letter and connect your strengths to the school's emphasis (e.g., technology). This will let your potential employers know that you have researched the school, that you are knowledgeable about the environment, and that you are selective in sending applications.

Format and appearance are important as they convey your professionalism. Consider the following, sometimes overlooked by busy candidates:

- Use quality bond paper and a matching envelope. White or very pale neutral shades are considered professional. Alternatively, consider a contemporary paper only if you think this may bring a positive reaction to your application.
- Verify that your printer is producing excellent copies. Crisp, clear type is essential.
- Identify and use the name of the principal, director of personnel, or an appropriate administrator in the inside address.
- Sign each letter above your printed name.

The résumé presents your experience and education as well as your special skills and abilities. For new teachers, it is usually one to two pages in length. It must be free of typographical errors and easy to read. Prospective employers look for specific information about you in a résumé. Call attention to your special characteristics. Make each category easy to locate and mark items you want to stand out with bullets. Table 4.1 provides information about the range of topics looked for in résumés.

Your name and contact information can be printed in a distinctive font that is both professional and attention getting, yet easy to read. Including your e-mail address implies that you are a competent computer user, an asset strongly valued in many schools.

Your prospective employer wants to know your teacher certification status. Note the anticipated date and title of the certification you are working toward. Use the accurate title of the certification as your state department of education specifies it.

The experience category is probably your best opportunity to distinguish yourself from other applicants while conveying your appropriateness for the position. Highlight and elaborate your specific successful experiences promoting children's learning—in student teaching, assistant teaching, internships, camp counseling, and tutoring.

The samples provided in Fig. 4.1 represent the experience sections of résumés submitted by Candidates A and B who are ap-

Table 4.1 Information to Include in Your Résumé

- Contact information
  - Your name
  - Address
  - Telephone number(s)
  - E-mail address [1]
  - Fax number
- Teacher certification status
- Educational background
  - Degree(s) and granting institutions
- Experience
  - In teaching
  - In other settings
- Special skills or interests
  - Music, sports, computer, travel, etc.
- References
- Professional credential file

[1]You will need to monitor your e-mail regularly to respond in a timely fashion as you do with telephone messages and surface mail.

Candidate A	
Experience in Teaching	**Student Teacher** Rose Avenue Elementary School September – December 2001 2nd grade Ms. M. Downs, Cooperating Teacher **Conducted lessons in Reading, Math, Social Studies and Science.** 5th Grade Ms. E. Lopez, Cooperating Teacher **Assisted the teacher in all curriculum lessons.**

Candidate B	
Experience in Teaching	**Student Teacher** Rose Avenue Elementary School September – December 2001 2nd grade Ms. M. Downs, Cooperating Teacher **Created and implemented a math learning center and evaluated its learning outcomes. Adapted lessons for different learning styles and abilities as well as multicultural differences within the class.** 5th Grade Ms. E. Lopez, Cooperating Teacher **Developed a thematic unit integrating curriculum, discovery learning, and cooperative activities in preparation for Earth Day. Established and tutored flexible groups in reading skills as needed.**

FIG. 4.1. Excerpts from sample résumés: Candidates A and B.

Which candidate is more likely to be called for an interview? Why?

plying for the same primary grade position. As you read them, consider the potential responses by members of a school selection committee.

Candidates C and D are applying to a school that is initiating an early childhood program. Read their experience sections in Fig. 4.2.

Candidates B and D provide details of classroom experience using strong action words depicting the writer as a planner, decision maker, organizer, and supervisor. Candidates A and C provide minimal information and do not distinguish themselves as unique and qualified.

The following are strong action words you may use to communicate your experiences and special strengths.

Organized	Initiated	Supervised
Presented	Improved	Chaired
Developed	Trained	Planned
Established	Coordinated	Restructured
Designed	Accomplished	Managed
Led	Enabled	Introduced
Conducted	Directed	Facilitated
Implemented	Researched	Devised

Select four action words and develop phrases that convey your experiences and strengths:

1.

2.

3.

4.

Special skills and interests can be a powerful, distinguishing category on your résumé. Did you coach soccer or field sports? Are you a musician? Can you incorporate singing or instruments in your classroom? Can you use your travels to enrich your students' understanding of other cultures? Mentioning these activ-

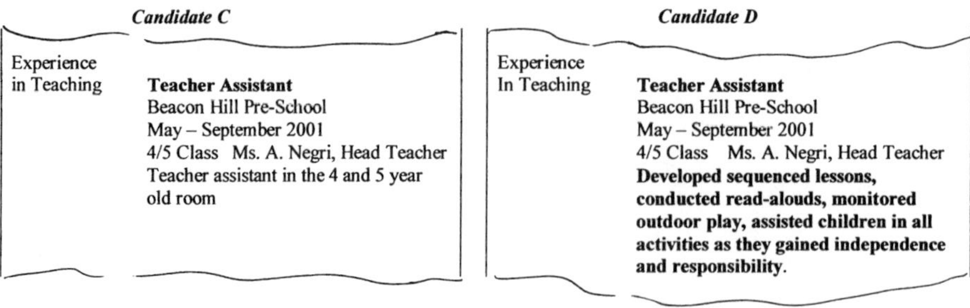
Candidate C

Experience in Teaching

Teacher Assistant
Beacon Hill Pre-School
May – September 2001
4/5 Class Ms. A. Negri, Head Teacher
Teacher assistant in the 4 and 5 year old room

Candidate D

Experience In Teaching

Teacher Assistant
Beacon Hill Pre-School
May – September 2001
4/5 Class Ms. A. Negri, Head Teacher
Developed sequenced lessons, conducted read-alouds, monitored outdoor play, assisted children in all activities as they gained independence and responsibility.

Which excerpt communicates an understanding of useful experiences for such a program?

FIG. 4.2. Excerpts from sample résumés: Candidates C and D.

ities might generate the school's interest in you, the goal you are seeking to achieve through your résumé.

The references section usually concludes the résumé and contains information about individuals who can corroborate your qualifications. There are several ways to provide references to a potential employer:

- If you have a credential file, provide the accurate name and address of the department and college or agency managing it so the school can access it easily.
- List names, addresses, phone numbers, e-mail addresses, and titles (cooperating teacher, principal, or professor of education) of people serving as references. Be sure that you ask permission to use the names of all those noted. Some schools will contact the persons you have listed in the references section of your résumé, requesting information over the telephone. You may create a separate page for references for easy access by the school.
- Attach letters of reference to your résumé when requested. Alternatively, you may end your résumé with a statement that references are available on request, or you may feel that it is taken for granted and such a notation offers no new information.

You will benefit from reading sample résumés in books that focus on that topic. Your teacher education career planning office is likely to have such materials. Keep in mind that your résumé is an advertisement that enhances your chances of being selected for an interview. Use all available resources to make it perfect.

OFFICIAL DOCUMENTS

In contrast to those documents you created independently, you will be asked for other materials over which you have little control: an application form, letters of recommendation, a credential file, and legal records.

Some schools require candidates to complete an application form even though a résumé has been submitted. This is an official document requesting prescribed information. You have control over your entries, but not over the categories of information requested. Therefore, the application form is a combination of a personally created document and an official document. The completed form provides the search committee with access to specific information in a standard format for easy review and comparison and for accurate data entry.

Completing an application form after constructing your résumé is a simple task because much of the same information is requested. As you respond to a job announcement, you might request an application form in advance of your interview. In some settings, there is a school policy requiring that you complete the application form at the time of the interview. In that case, bring a copy of your résumé for reference, and fill in all blanks on the form. "See résumé" is not an appropriate response. Be careful to print legibly and proofread the final document before you submit it. Neatness, accuracy, and adherence to the directions are evaluated in considering your application.

Some schools ask candidates to include letters of recommendation with their résumé. You may photocopy letters you have gathered and bring additional copies to the interview, making it easy for each interviewer to read about you. You may also state that you will have your college credential file sent. Although you have no control over what may be communicated in a recommendation, you do have control in identifying references. Select cooperating teachers, supervisors, professors, and principals who know about your qualifications, who have seen you teach, and who are likely to be positive. Using a credential file may spare your references the necessity of sending multiple letters on your behalf. We discuss credential files next.

During your teacher education program, you may ask for a letter of recommendation when you complete an early field experience or a particularly engaging course. Before you leave your placement as student teacher, assistant teacher, or intern, ask the principal and teachers with whom you have worked for recommendation letters or for permission to use their names as references. Of course, this is appropriate only if they have seen you engaging in professional activities.

Many college career placement offices provide services to their graduating students that include the establishment of a professional credential file. This file is an organized collection of documents that some prospective employers may request, or the file may be forwarded on your request. Typically, a credential file includes a completed placement office information form, recommendations, transcripts, and copies of certifications.

NOTES NOTES NOTES

You may have a confidential or a nonconfidential file. A confidential file is one in which you waive your right to review letters of recommendation and other materials placed in your file. A nonconfidential file is open for your review. The placement office supplies a recommendation form containing an option to waive your right to see the completed recommendation. If you waive your right, the remarks are confidential and perceived as more candid than comments that can be read by the candidate. Be sure to investigate your options and the policies of the career placement office thoroughly before you establish your credential file.

Some college placement offices are computerizing this service. They may send your file to the requesting school by fax or e-mail. In addition, independent Web-based credentials management companies, such as Interfolio.com, now offer this service directly to candidates.

Once you have taken the time to establish a credential file, keep it updated by adding current references, transcripts, and résumés. The benefit of a credential file extends to the people you use as references. If you request a letter for your file, they will be spared the necessity of submitting the same letter to several schools. The placement office facilitates the process by reproducing your recommendations and sending them to prospective employers. Using your credential file frees you of worries about any delays in individual responses from your references.

Your legal records (academic degrees, teacher certifications, driver's license, Social Security card) may be required when a school employs you. Some schools request you submit copies as part of the application process, whereas others defer requesting those materials until the hiring decision is made. You may be asked to bring your originals to the interview.

SUMMING UP

> If you don't tell the school about your strong qualifications, who will? Dizzy Dean, of baseball fame, said, "It ain't braggin' if you dun it [sic]."

The documents described in this chapter communicate who you are to your prospective employer. If you don't tell the school about your strong qualifications, who will? It is your opportunity, and responsibility, and in your best interest, to communicate your assets. It is also in the best interest of the school to have comprehensive information about you during the hiring deliberations. Do all you can to help them to know you. Your next step is to prepare to discuss in detail every item in your documents.

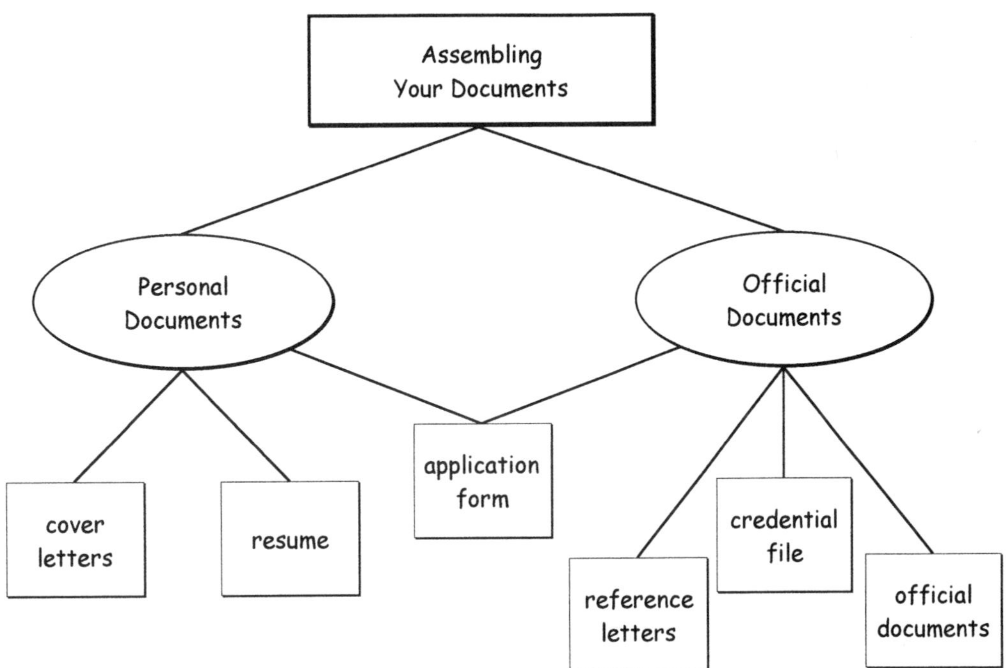

PART C

KNOWING THE PROCESS

Schools use many types of screening activities to evaluate candidates. Some are similar to those used in business; others are unique to schools and teaching. Becoming familiar with the various settings you may encounter can preclude unnecessary stress. Felicia has been invited to return for a second interview during which she will engage in a role-play situation involving an irate parent. We note how she addresses the issues that confront her, as a way of preparing for your potential interactions at interviews.

Chapter 5, Exploring Screening Activities, introduces many common formats used for selecting teachers, and explores diverse contexts, contents, and processes.

Once at the interview it is essential that you understand the questions posed by interviewers. In Chapter 6, Interpreting Interviewers' Questions, we consider interviewers' predictable questions, interpreting the information they are implicitly seeking as a guide to planning your own responses.

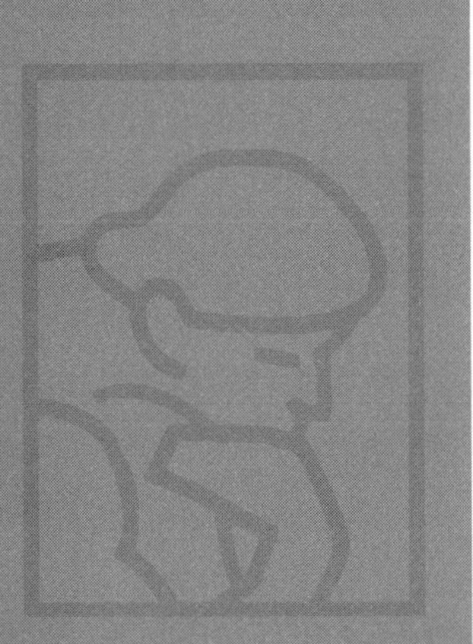

Scenario:	Felicia Gunderson A Second, School-Based Interview With a Role Play
Chapter 5	Exploring Screening Activities
Chapter 6	Interpreting Interviewers' Questions

SCENARIO

FELICIA GUNDERSON

A Second, School-Based Interview With a Role Play

Candidate:	Felicia Gunderson	
Interviewers:	Mrs. Jeffers	Principal (who also role plays as a parent, Mrs. Jones)
	Mrs. Dolan	Parent
	Mrs. Acosta	Fourth-Grade Teacher

Many schools conduct at least two interviews with potential candidates. The initial interview may include the principal, the assistant principal, and a teacher. Based on their recommendations, a second interview may be arranged to include at least one parent and another teacher. This second interview may be more intense. Felicia is appearing for a second interview at the Spencer Elementary School and she knows it will include a role play.

Because of the heavy influence of parents at Spencer, the staff decided to standardize a parent–teacher role play as a part of the second-level screening. The principal takes the role of the parent in a prepared script. This is the context in which Felicia finds herself. She's meeting again with Mrs. Jeffers along with two new people, a fourth-grade teacher and a parent. She's been successful up to this point and she hopes a second interview will advance her chances of getting a position.

WHO IS FELICIA?

Felicia was asked by Joan, a friend, to fill in as a summer counselor in camp. "What? Fill in? Give up my vacation? I'd only do this for a good friend," she said. Reflecting on her experiences, Felicia learned something about herself at camp. She discovered that she really liked children and she discovered that she might be good at working with them. Although she was successful in her job and enjoyed what she was doing, she often felt there was something missing. After her month-long tenure as camp counselor, she decided to enroll in a master's in teaching program to prepare for a teaching career. We meet Felicia after 8 months in that year-long program, as she is seeking a full-time teaching post.

She brings to the interview and to the field of teaching strengths that enabled her to succeed in the corporate world. She is confident and she's mature. She knows when to ask questions, and she knows how to clarify information. Interviews don't really scare Felicia; on one level she actually welcomes the opportunity to talk. She was always the one asked by colleagues to represent them at meetings. She "knows" people and considers herself a good communicator. She prepared for the second meeting by identifying key elements in her background: her course work, her student teaching, her own high school and college years, and the previous positions she held.

As she researched the district over the Internet, she discovered interesting information made available by the state education department. She concluded that the taxpayers of Rochford School District value education, participate in the day-to-day activities of the school, and regularly approve school budgets. Felicia believes the district's priorities and her strengths appear to be a good match.

She made sure her portfolio was in good order. Felicia asked during the phone call inviting her back if there was a precedent for bringing materials to the interview. The personnel secretary told her that most principals in the district welcome anything that might help them to know the candidate. She feels ready.

She is well into the interview when we hear the dialogue. Mrs. Jeffers has been reviewing Felicia's portfolio as they've been talking. As she places the portfolio on the table we tune into their conversation.

THE INTERVIEW

What are some issues you would discuss in responding to a question about a child-centered curriculum?

Mrs. Jeffers: Thank you, Felicia, for bringing your portfolio with you. It's quite impressive. I particularly like your mission statement outlining your philosophy of a child-centered classroom. We have classes of 25 to 28 students here at Spencer Elementary, and we are interested to know how you would enact a "child at the center of the curriculum" philosophy in a first-grade class, for example.

Felicia: Well, as you can see from some of the photos in my portfolio, I did much of my student teaching in large classes and I don't see any reason why child centeredness and large classes can't go together. There are many ways to address the child as the focus of the classroom. (Felicia opens her portfolio to a tabbed page with captioned photos of reading time.) [1]

What are your personal strengths that you might call on as indicators of your philosophy of education?

First, you need to be super organized for any class to run smoothly. You need a system for hanging up coats, a signal for quiet, and another for movement throughout the room, and you need to get this going very early in the year. These systems need to be fully understood by all the students and consistently carried out by the teacher. All this has to be introduced and practiced early in the school year.

Another way to bolster child centeredness in large classrooms is individualized programs. One instructional program I like in particular is Reading Recovery. I did my student teaching in a first-grade class where Reading Recovery was in place. It's an early intervention program which identifies first graders who need a little extra help as emergent readers. These struggling readers are put in a one-to-one situation with a reading teacher for 30 minutes each day for a limited number of weeks, perhaps 10 to 14 weeks. At the end of the year, many of the children go into mainstream second-grade reading programs. Programs like this allow teachers to keep the child at the center of the curriculum. These are a few ways to have a child-centered curriculum and maybe, if we have time later, I could talk about a few more ways. [2]

Compare your list above with those issues Felicia addressed.

KEEP IN MIND

[1]Felicia reinforces her experiences in large classes with pictures. She was able to prepare for such a question because her research on the district revealed information about class size. Her philosophy of child centeredness and her beliefs about teaching and learning in her mission statement provide the basis for her response to Mrs. Jeffers's question.

[2]When Felicia says, "You need to be super organized," she projects an image that she's in charge. She is organized and knowledgeable. It is unclear if her research on the district uncovered any specific programs in practice, but she has "heard" the question and responds with the discussion of Reading Recovery, displaying knowledge of current reading programs that might be appropriate for Spencer Elementary. She uses her portfolio to segue into the child-centered curriculum, including her ideas about organization and classroom management. Teaching a class of 25 to 28 students requires a great deal of preparation and planning, and Felicia assures Mrs. Jeffers that she's aware that she will have to use all her skills to run an effective classroom.

THE ROLE PLAY

Try your hand at preparing for a role play in an interview. Identify problem situations to address with each of the following pairs:

- *teacher – student*
- *teacher – parent*
- *teacher – teacher*
- *teacher – administrator*

Mrs. Dolan (parent): Thank you Felicia, I'd like to hear more, but I think we'll start that role play you were told about when you were called back for this second interview. *(Reading from a script)* Our district is known to be one with a high tax rate and very involved parents. Mrs. Jeffers, our principal, will take the role of Mrs. Jones, the mother of Johnny. As we told you on the telephone, the role play will be about a parent who is not happy with the teacher who changed her child's seat. Let's start. [3]

Mrs. Jones, parent (Mrs. Jeffers): Well, I got into my car and raced over here the minute Johnny got off the school bus in tears. [Indignant] What is the meaning of changing his seat? He was very happy with the children he was sitting with.

Felicia: Mrs. Jones, may I say I'm delighted to have Johnny in my class. He adds such humor and exuberance to the classroom and he's wonderfully kind to other children.

Create your own opening remarks that will accomplish the following points:

- *Open the conversation with a positive statement about the student.*
- *Assure parents that you recognize the child's good qualities.*
- *Try to calm an irate mother and bring her into a more reasonable state so she can "hear" more clearly.*

Mrs. Jones, parent (Mrs. Jeffers): Well that's nice to hear.

Felicia: I think I can explain the present situation but may I ask you for your understanding of the events just to make sure we're on the same page. [4]

Mrs. Jones, parent (Mrs. Jeffers): He got off the bus saying that you changed his table for no reason. He liked the boys—he even liked the girls at Table 3. Now he's all the way at Table 6 and he's most unhappy, and frankly I don't think you handled this very well.

Felicia: Mrs. Jones, I can appreciate your concern but I honestly thought I could prevent this from escalating, and I was on my way to the telephone to call you when I saw you entering the building. As you know, Johnny is a very bright child but he tends to be extremely active. He jumps up in his chair when he

---

KEEP IN MIND

[3]Felicia expected that there would be a parent on the panel and she responded to the request to participate in a role play just as she would have responded to a request for a writing sample or a demonstration lesson. It didn't surprise her.

[4]Felicia asked for the parent's perspective so there could be no mistake that all parties were speaking about the same topic. She intends to assure Mrs. Jones that whatever is going on, all concerned (teacher, student, and parent) will try to arrive at a mutually agreeable solution. She communicates that she is interested in the psychological, intellectual, social, and physical well-being of Johnny and every other child in the room.

wants attention, he calls out, and sometimes he even falls off his chair and topples into other children. [5]

Mrs. Jones, parent (Mrs. Jeffers): I'm sure that other children behave the same way. It's not only Johnny.

Felicia: It happens that the other children at Table 3 are quite subdued and that was part of the reason I placed him there. I thought he might influence them and they him. It didn't work out that way.

I took Johnny aside at recess last week and tried talking with him and he seemed to understand. We talked about how his calling out and jumping up disturbed the other children. When I asked him what we could do and how we might solve the problem, it was Johnny who came up with the idea of changing seats.

Mrs. Jones, parent (Mrs. Jeffers): I want him back at his original table.

Felicia: On Monday I told him that his behavior was still bothering other children and we would have to do something about his seat. There was no change in behavior and today he even went so far as to hit Janine. At this point it was 2:30 in the afternoon when I "walked" him over to another table and said we would discuss it tomorrow.

Mrs. Jones, parent (Mrs. Jeffers): Well, he certainly shouldn't be hitting people.

Felicia: Mrs. Jones, do you remember our last parent–teacher conference when we talked about Johnny's behavior? I have it here in my log that we were both going to keep an eye on it. You kept referring to him as rambunctious, saying "Boys will be boys." I believe that children need physical outlets for their energies and it seems that Johnny is very active, so I've been thinking of ways we might channel Johnny's enthusiasm—outside of school as well as inside. [6]

NOTES NOTES NOTES

What are some positive steps Felicia has taken to show that she is capable of dealing with a parent who is upset at something happening in Felicia's classroom?

How would you tell a parent that his or her wishes will not be immediately satisfied?

What would you enter in your log about your interaction with Mrs. Jones?

KEEP IN MIND

[5]Felicia comments on Johnny's strengths, assuring his mother that he is a bright child. She gets to the purpose of the meeting: Johnny's behavior is unsafe for Johnny and his classmates.

[6]Felicia is confronted with a parent intent on accomplishing what she came for; that is, to have her child returned to his original place. Felicia is focusing on the reasons for the change and sees it is important to make Mrs. Jones aware of all the particulars that led to the decision: Other students are in physical danger, Johnny is in danger, and she intended to make a phone call if it couldn't be resolved in the classroom. *(continued)*

NOTES NOTES NOTES

Mrs. Jones, parent (Mrs. Jeffers): I believe children need physical outlets, too.

Felicia: A new gymnastics club is starting next week here at school and many girls and boys are interested in signing up. Perhaps you would like it for Johnny as well. Also the physical education teacher tells me Johnny is a superior runner. Could we arrange for him to try out for the junior track team? In class I'll scout out more ways to use his enthusiasm, as in extra "jobs."

I'm sorry Johnny was upset, Mrs. Jones, and I certainly don't want you or him to be unhappy, but for the present and for the safety of Johnny and all the other students, we'll keep him at Table 6. We'll talk about table changes in a couple of days. We've made him aware of how his exuberance is affecting others and now we all—you and Johnny and I—can start working on it. Other than this, Johnny is developing nicely in so many ways.

What are three important ways in which Felicia attempted to solve the problem of an unruly child?

Mrs. Jones, parent (Mrs. Jeffers): Well, all right, I can see how you're trying to teach him a lesson. But I want him back at his original table as soon as possible.

Felicia: Great, Mrs. Jones, and thank you so much for coming in to help straighten this out. Let's be in touch by phone next week. [7]

Mrs. Jeffers: *(Returning to her role as principal and interviewer)* Thank you, Felicia, for taking the role of teacher. You handled it very well. And thank you for coming in for a second interview. We'll get back to you as soon as we begin to make decisions.

KEEP IN MIND

Felicia kept a record of conversations with parents that enables her to refer to past agreements. The log helped her to detail the history of the present situation. The log can be an important memory aid, especially when teachers have 25 to 28 students to think about.

[7]Felicia was responsive to the mother's concern, letting her know she heard what the parent was saying. She was careful not to put Mrs. Jones on the defensive because solutions are difficult to arrive at when one party is angry and not listening. Felicia identified the steps that preceded her decision to move Johnny. Her actions reflect her philosophy of helping students to think critically and keeping them at the center of the curriculum. She was successful in focusing on the incident, while emphasizing the positive attributes of the child. She left Johnny's mother with the impression that they would talk in the near future and that Johnny would be returned to his seat just as soon as his behavior no longer proved a threat to the safety of himself and the other children.

SUMMING UP

Felicia presented a clear picture of her special qualities: She is a caring person, experienced with large classes and child-oriented teaching and learning. As she reflected on the questions and her responses, she was pleased but regretted that she was not more thorough in discussing classroom management. She might have included the physical setting of her ideal classroom as well as her philosophy about including students in the governance of the class. She could have discussed her ideas about rewards and consequences. Felicia will rewrite her response to a question about classroom organization to include these important points and she will rehearse it to ensure that she remembers it for her next interview.

Felicia is an articulate young woman who is confident about who she is, knowledgeable and capable of managing a classroom. Planning to call on her strength of organization often during her teaching career, she conveys a caring, child-oriented attitude, eager to solve problems. With her energetic understanding, especially when it comes to children's needs, she displays a "can do" demeanor that would be welcomed by most administrators.

She was proud of her role-play performance and she was very happy that she was able to recall the incident that actually happened when she took over a class at the end of last term. She was delighted that she rehearsed it and was able to enact the scene during her interview. In reviewing her mnemonic of the characteristics she hoped to convey during the interview, she concluded that she was quite successful. She was happy she made the decision to become an educator.

E – Eager, energetic
D – Dedicated
U – Understanding, untiring
C – Child oriented, confident
A – Articulate, able
T – Thoughtful
O – Organized, open
R – Resourceful

CHAPTER 5

EXPLORING SCREENING ACTIVITIES

AT A GLANCE

We focus on four major screening activities:

- Interviews.
- Teaching performance.
- Materials review.
- Evaluation processes.

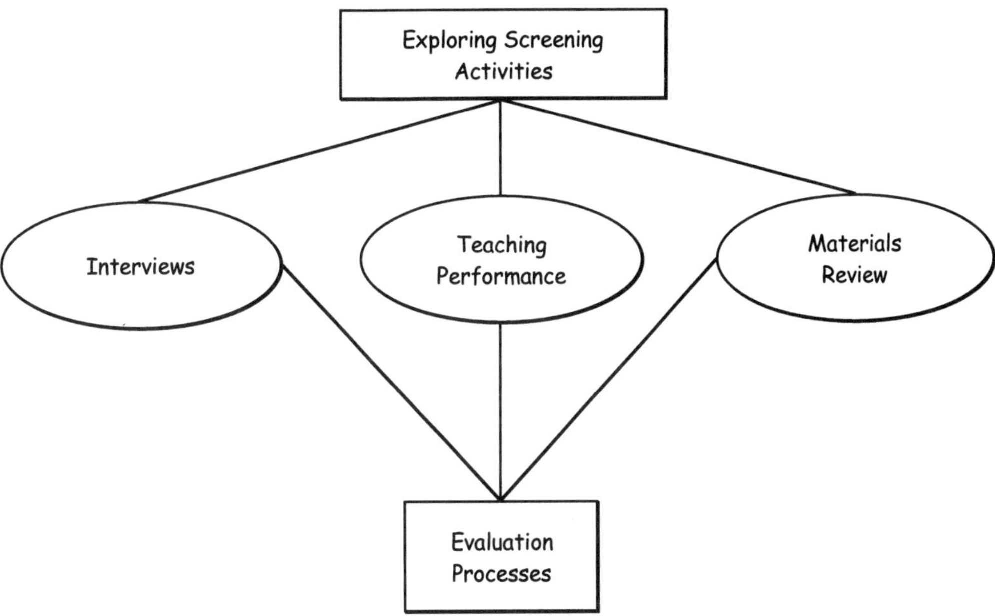

The complex screening process is influenced by numerous factors: scope of the search, number of applicants, and educational goals. Although screening activities vary greatly in form, they provide the opportunity for you to convey important characteristics that may result in a positive decision for you. Table 5.1 notes some of these.

Table 5.1 Characteristics Considered in Screening

- Your voice and communication skills
- Your social interaction skills
- Your appearance
- The depth and breadth of your academic and professional knowledge and experience
- Your commitment and emotional readiness for teaching
- Your confidence as shown in this setting and with these players

Every contact, even the most casual one, contributes to the decision-making process. For example, your voice and communication skills (dialect, fluency, confidence) will be evaluated when you telephone to verify receipt of your application or respond to a request for further information. Your social skills and confidence can be observed in your brief comments to a secretary, during your phone conversation, and during your formal interview. Your knowledge of liberal arts, science, and pedagogy are assessed in your in-depth interview as well as in your demonstration lesson. Your skills at interacting with students may be evaluated through a videotaped lesson or demonstration lesson. You should consider informal (casual) conversation as well as formal interviews as part of the screening process.

INTERVIEWS

The most frequently used screening activity, the interview, is often the most unpredictable. These person-to-person interactions differ in many ways, influenced by who the participants are, how they are seated, and how questions are posed, among other variables. The school governance influences the interview format. You may have multiple interviews culminating in one with a senior administrator or the superintendent of schools. You may meet as many as 10 people serving on the selection committee. Or the principal or a member of the school selection committee may be the only person to interview you. You may have sequential interviews; that is, brief screenings with one or more persons after which you may be brought immediately to a more senior person for an in-depth interview or you may be finished for that day. You may find yourself invited for multiple interviews, or you may receive a job offer after one interview.

The range of potential **participants** at an interview is evident in our scenarios with Steve, Jennifer, Felicia, Marcy, and Kippi. We present various combinations for you to consider: single candidate, multiple candidates, single interviewer, and multiple interviewers.

A single candidate with a single interviewer, as in Steve's case, is the most common form of interview. A one-to-one interview may range from a brief, perfunctory glance at you to a lengthy questioning of your educational understandings, strategies, and experiences. You may meet with a member of the selection committee as a preliminary screening to determine if you will be invited back for other levels of evaluation, or you may have an in-depth interview with a principal or other decision maker. The location can be an office setting or a gymnasium job fair where you wait until a screener is available to talk with you for a few minutes. Many job fair interviews are little more than opportunities to submit résumés and be evaluated for appearance and speech.

Multiple candidates may be interviewed at the same time, all seeking the same position. Often the interviewers ask the candidates the same questions and go around the table until all have completed their answers. This competitive setting emphasizes distinguishing yourself from other candidates. Listen carefully to their comments while contemplating ways to promote your own candidacy.

Multiple interviewers meet with a single candidate when there are several schools in a district with openings. Individually, principals conduct initial screenings. After the pool has been reduced, they collectively interview the candidate, each principal seeking the best match to fit his or her school.

There may be one or more interviewer(s) who reflect the range of influential voices in a school district (e.g., administrators, parents, teachers, and other staff members). They may represent one school where the opening exists, several schools in the district, or personnel from the central office. In all of these situations, your actions will be scrutinized and documented for later evaluation.

The two most frequently used **interview settings** are meeting together or meeting remotely through technology.

When meeting together, you are likely to be directed to a room where you will meet the interviewer(s). The physical setting in this room contributes to your perception of the style of the school. Regardless of whether the setting appears austere or cozy, remember that the atmosphere is created by the interaction among those present, including you. Readily offer a cordial, firm handshake. Your preference may be to sit across the desk from a principal and chat about your qualifications, but you could find yourself at a conference table or in a more formal setting. Be prepared to quickly adjust to the setting and focus on your interviewer(s) to communicate clearly and directly. Figure 5.1 represents some typical settings for meeting together.

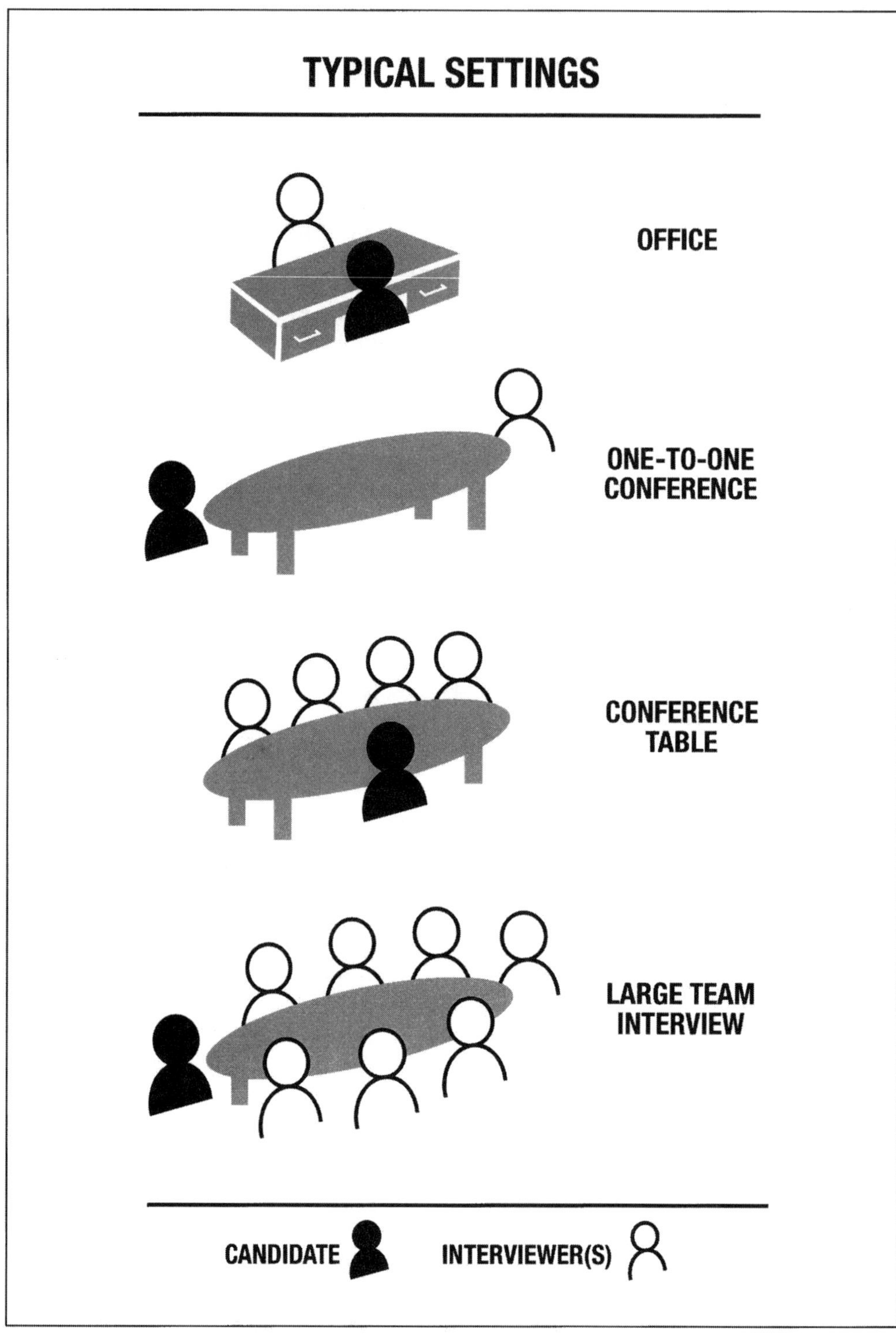

FIG. 5.1. Typical interview settings.

Meeting through technology serves to expedite interviewing, a major emphasis in much of the selection process. Some school personnel conduct their initial screenings by telephone, particularly when there are too many candidates to invite for lengthy in-person interviews. School personnel pose the same questions they would ask when actually sitting with you in the same room.

NOTES NOTES NOTES

Schools considering applicants who reside a distance from the school find that teleconferencing is an efficient, economic tool. By scheduled appointment, the interviewer(s) and the candidate have a virtual meeting and exchange information. In this process, you are able to see each other, perhaps even displaying photographs from your portfolio, while all parties scrutinize the goodness of fit. Appointments to use teleconferencing facilities are made at nearby institutions or commercial services that have online capacity. Districts that utilize this technology will refer you to convenient locations for your "meeting." A successful interview may result in an appointment for in-person meetings or perhaps a demonstration lesson, limiting the number of candidates flown in to meet the selection committee, expediting the process, and reducing the cost.

Types of interactions during an interview can range from responsive to structured to semistructured. Districts may choose spontaneous exchanges or they may prefer to use predetermined questions or topics. There may be an explicit statement describing the interview style or you may need to infer the type of interview being used.

Responsive interviews, the style most frequently used in our scenarios, are collaborative conversations. They draw on personal characteristics noted in your résumé that prompted the scheduling of your interview or on the specific needs of the school. The reactions of the interviewers enable you to judge whether your comments have been understood and when you should elaborate on particular topics. It is the give-and-take of conversation that is the essential quality in these interactions. In chapters 6, 7, and 8 you will practice answering questions that are typically incorporated in responsive interviews.

In addition, there may be some opportunities for other types of performances. In her scenario, Felicia was asked to engage in a role-play situation. You might encounter such an opportunity as well. In role playing you are likely to be provided with some preliminary background information about a typical situation or conflict. In your designated role you interact with others who assume the role(s) of members of the school community (students, parents, teachers, and staff). Use this opportunity to demonstrate your interpersonal skills, your professionalism, and your ability to solve problem situations.

Another example of an activity at a responsive interview is the dialog that may emerge as you present your portfolio to support and illustrate your responses to various questions. In chapter 9 we suggest strategies to prepare for possible role-play requests and for organizing and presenting your portfolio. Although responsive interviews are pervasive, other formats are becoming more common. We turn to these now.

Structured interviews may increase objectivity and be expedient. Some schools choose to conduct structured interviews in which the same prescripted questions are posed to each candidate.

One example of structured interviews is behavioral interviewing, as in the Gallup Organization's perceiver interview test. It consists of a series of commercially developed questions focusing on candidates' professional behaviors. The candidate's responses in the behavioral interview are compared to the school's predetermined, preferred answers. Behavioral interviews are typically administered early in the screening process.

Another example of a structured interview is the automated or computerized screening questionnaire, which may be used as an initial screening activity. On receipt of your cover letter and résumé, the district may send you information about the automated screening and provide a telephone number to call or a Web site to access. After identifying yourself, you listen to or read the questions and respond by using the telephone keypad or the computer keyboard. Responses are compiled by computer and the results are available to the district in a matter of hours. Both of these formats are frequently used as first-level evaluation processes to reduce the candidate pool to those aligned with the district's values.

Another variety of structured interview restricts the in-person interviewers to the use of prescripted questions. When there are multiple interviewers, each agrees to ask one or two of the specified questions. This process gives no opportunity for dialog to expand on incomplete or vague answers. By design, the interviewers may not follow up on your response. In such a scenario they proceed to the next question when you complete your response. Consequently you are responsible for assuring that your first answer is complete, responsive, and conveys your strong credentials.

A semistructured interview is a combination of structured and responsive formats. Interviewers may address an issue or topic in personalized language or as predetermined, prescripted questions. They may respond to your comments by asking additional, spontaneous questions and they may ask follow-up questions based on your remarks. These semistructured interviews offer a balance between structured and spontaneous interactions.

TEACHING PERFORMANCE

The screening process may include some or all of the following: a demonstration lesson, an observation as you work as an assistant teacher or student teacher, or your performance during substitute teaching. These activities give the screening committee valuable information with which to evaluate your proficiencies in the more practical aspects of teaching, for example, organizing a class for learning and implementing your beliefs about teaching. Some districts request that you provide a videotape of yourself teaching. The tape is then included as part of your materials review.

In a **demonstration lesson** the district may ask you to teach a brief lesson to assess your planning skills, your creativity, your understanding of curriculum, your interaction with students, and your confidence and poise. Knowing the length of time available, the grade level of the class, the number of students, and some of the topics they have been studying will help in your preparation. It is appropriate to ask for such information when it is not provided, showing that you recognize the necessity of incorporating the students' characteristics into each lesson. You may provide your lesson plan to the observer(s). Acknowledge to yourself that this is an artificial context, not one where any significant learning is likely to occur. In preparation, you might refer to Kippi's scenario, which includes a demonstration lesson.

As an **assistant teacher or student teacher**, there have been numerous opportunities for informal observations by the school community. You may request the interview committee to formally observe your teaching. They may request information from your head teacher regarding your ability to promote academic growth.

You have had the daily opportunity to communicate your strengths as an effective teacher in real classroom interactions with students who know you. You are in a unique position to gauge student progress and modify instruction. Be prepared to showcase projects your students participated in under your direction as well as some concrete evidence of your planning and preparation. As a member of the staff you can inquire about openings. In addition, you should frequently remind the administration about your desire to teach in this school.

As a **substitute teacher** you have the opportunity of being chosen for a school staff based, in large measure, on your performance during a substitute assignment. As you register for the substitute list, make inquiries about any information accessible to substitutes. Ask for permission to tour the building and spend time talking to staff about any curriculum projects they may be conducting. In your enthusiasm and desire to prepare, be cautious not to annoy anyone.

Knowing about the school and the students will enable you to build a repertoire of teaching strategies. Your inquiries will form a basis for developing generic lessons as you prepare to substitute teach. Subbing allows the administration and staff to see, firsthand, some of your abilities working with students, and it gives you instant information about the school culture.

MATERIALS REVIEW

Your videotaped lesson, writing sample, test scores, and grades all provide information to help the district with its hiring decision. Make sure these materials are of the highest quality and that they broadcast your unique characteristics to future employers.

If you are asked for a **videotaped lesson**, you may submit it with a lesson plan or other explanation of your goals and strategies. It is reasonable to expect that you will identify the student growth and learning you hope will be accomplished in this activity. The advantage of a video is that it could, as part of a long-term activity you are working on with your students, demonstrate your considered reasons for your educational decisions.

There are ethical concerns about videotaping or photographing students in school. Be sure that you follow your school's policy. If you are unable to videotape students, explain this to your potential employer.

A spontaneous **writing sample** is required by many districts in their screening process. Some districts inform candidates about the criteria for evaluation, such as fluency, organization, correct usage, and creativity. The writing sample may be asked for early in the screening process, or it may be requested when the candidate pool has been reduced by other screening activities. Groups of candidates may be assembled and provided with an instruction sheet identifying suggested topics and noting the time available for writing (see Fig. 5.2).

Test scores and grades document the content knowledge of prospective teachers. Some districts require standardized scores, some collect college transcripts noting the grade point average, and some administer their own competency tests in various subject areas. Most states require candidates to take teacher certification exams developed by educators of that state or by a national evaluation company. The purpose of these examinations is to help ensure that certified teachers have the knowledge, skills, and dispositions that the state considers important. One test used by many states is The Praxis Series, an Educational

REQUEST FOR WRITING SAMPLE

To The Candidate:

You will have 30 minutes to plan and write an essay on one of the topics below. You may write only on the assigned topic. Make sure to give specific examples to support your thesis. Proof read your essay carefully and take care to express your ideas clearly and effectively.

1. **In the last 20 years, the deterioration of the environment has become a growing concern among both scientists and ordinary citizens. Choose one pressing environmental problem, explain its negative impact, and discuss possible solutions.**

2. **"That government is best which governs least". Do you agree or disagree with this statement? Choose a specific example from current events, personal experience, or your reading to support your position.**

FIG. 5.2. Typical instruction sheet for writing sample.

Testing Service (ETS) program. Three categories of assessments in The Praxis Series are designed to correspond to your development as a teacher.

There are resources to help you prepare for each of the exams, some developed by the test makers and others created within the commercial test preparation community, for example, Barron's Test Preparation Series. ETS offers study guides, test preparation kits, books of general information, practice tests, and study tips. ETS can be reached on line at www.teachingandlearning.com or by mail at ETS, P.O. Box 6051, Princeton, NJ 08541-6051. State tests have corresponding preparation materials.

EVALUATION PROCESSES

You will wonder how a district makes choices during the screening activities. How will you be evaluated? The district has accumulated a wealth of information about you as a teacher: your materials, your teaching performance, and your interview. Throughout the screening they are conducting on-going evaluation based on criteria reflecting the style and needs of the district. One example may be the informal notes jotted down by Mr. Erickson during Steve's interview and later shared conversationally with others (see Fig. 5.3).

Pro	Con
Recommended by valued colleagues	Little experience
Enthusiastic - Ready and willing	Vague sense of class activities and organization
Articulate	
Resourceful	Might expect me to tell him what to do
Knowledgeable - standards, curriculum mapping	No recent books read - but papers & magazines

FIG. 5.3. Sample notes from Steve's interview.

Districts frequently create standard procedures to use with all candidates; some may be more formal than others. We list some typical formats for reflection followed by two sample interview evaluations as exemplars of the total evaluation process. You may extrapolate from these formats in understanding the range of protocols used by districts.

Formal	Informal
Checklist observation form	Post interview discussion notes
Interview evaluation form	Post observation votes
Rank order of preference sheet	Brief written comments
Rubric portfolio evaluation	

A formal evaluation instrument for a structured or semi-structured interview may include the questions, topics, and space for quantifying each interviewer's perceptions (see Fig. 5.4 and Fig. 5.5). Whether the evaluations are formal or informal they are intended to provide objective comparisons in the deliberation process. Eventually you are compared to other applicants. Because all these procedures involve human beings, personal perceptions and biases may influence the evaluations.

Interview Rating Sheet

Candidate ______________________ **Interviewer** ______________________

Question	Very Strong (1)	Rating Strong (2)	Fair (3)	Weak (4)	Very Weak (5)
1. Tell us a little about yourself.					
Notes:					
2. Why are you anxious to get a job here? Why should we hire you?					
Notes:					
3. Can you describe the classroom you might create if we hired you? What would it look like?					
Notes:					

Summary Evaluation

Invite to Next Level **Hold for Possible Consideration** **Does Not Match District's Needs. Send Thank You Letter**

FIG. 5.4. Sample evaluation form for structured interviews.

INTERVIEW EVALUATION FORM

Name of Candidate______________________________

Date______________________________________

Personal Characteristics	Notes		
	Strong	Average	Weak
Communication/Speech			
Professional Knowledge			
Organization/Management			
Presence/Demeanor			

Recommendation: **Reasons:**

Interviewer Signature

____

FIG. 5.5. Sample evaluation form for responsive interviews.

SUMMING UP

Whether your screening is done by one person or a committee, for 5 minutes or 30 minutes, in a conversational give-and-take or in a prescripted format, practice and preparation will increase your confidence. The number of interviewers, the style of interview, and the physical setting are variables you will encounter during the search. Because evaluations are subject to a variety of influences, familiarity with the possible types of screening activities enables you to be prepared for many eventualities.

Usually many individuals participate in the selection process with multiple opportunities to observe you. Ultimately they will decide if you fit into the style of their school. You, too, are attentively gathering information and contemplating whether you will be comfortable and able to function well as a colleague in this placement. You may want to create evaluation forms of your own on which you note a district's match to your needs. You and the school both want to find the match that benefits the students you will teach.

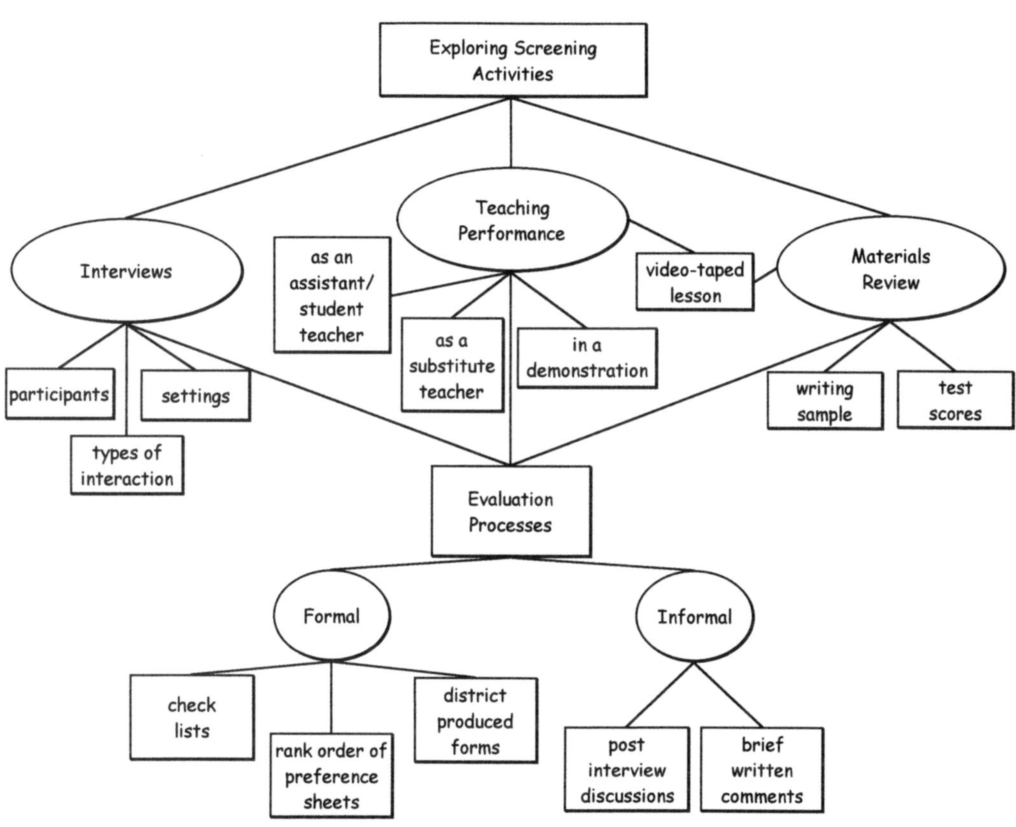

CHAPTER 6

INTERPRETING INTERVIEWERS' QUESTIONS

AT A GLANCE

This chapter will jump-start your understanding of questions that are typically presented at interviews and how interviewers seek similar information using different terms and phrases. In this process we help you to analyze each request, identify multiple issues being addressed, and organize your ideas for an articulate response.

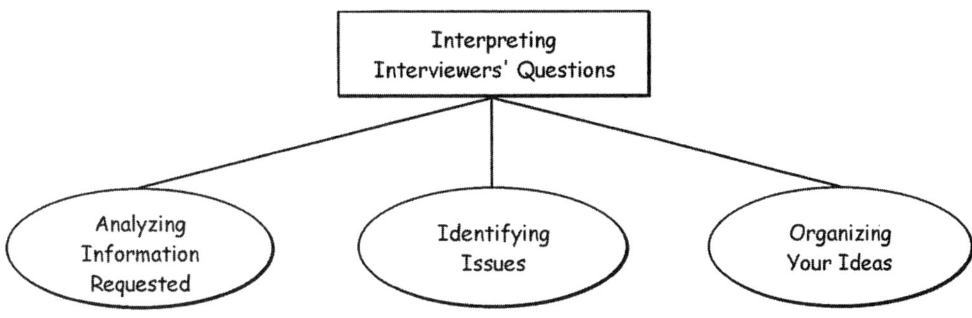

We next present seven issues that are typically addressed in interviews, although in very different ways. The process will help you to analyze interviewers' requests, identify the issues, and organize your ideas. We pose several versions of questions in each cluster; the underlined words contain the essence of the request. Your first step is to analyze each cluster looking for the primary purpose of the questions. Are you being asked about your credentials or your philosophy? Does the question address classroom experience or personal characteristics that can affect the school community? Is your knowledge of how children learn being addressed, or does the question relate to your knowledge of current curriculum standards? Take time to identify the issue and relate it to the realities of the particular school setting. Now you are ready to connect the purpose, the issue, and your ideas. Identify items in your list of qualifications that relate to the issue addressed. Organize the ideas that you would include in your response. Such note taking is the first step in developing appropriate responses.

PRACTICE ISSUE 1

YOURSELF

Tell us about yourself.

Please introduce yourself.

To open this interview why don't you tell us a little about your background?

What special characteristics do you bring to a school, a classroom, and students?

The interviewer may seek to use this as an ice-breaker, allowing you to settle into the session and to get to know more about you than is presented in your résumé. Your answer will reveal important information such as your:

- Educational priorities.
- Professional knowledge.
- Style of interaction.
- Speaking ability.
- Confidence.

By describing your experiences and qualifications in your introductory statement, you will establish that you are articulate and well prepared to fill the teaching opening. Take this opportunity to mention several experiences promoting your qualifications. Your interviewers may request greater detail. This strategy enables you to influence much of the conversation. Organize your preliminary thoughts in responding to these questions. For this first practice we list some topics you might wish to include in your notes along with some examples.

NOTES NOTES NOTES

Your Response
Educational Background

Certification Status

Experience Teaching

Experience With Children

Tutored

Counseling in summer day camp

Interests

Travel

Sports

Talents / Skills

Photography

Computer

PRACTICE ISSUE 2

LEARNING PRINCIPLES

Briefly tell us about your philosophy of education.

How do you define education?

Which learning theories have the greatest influence on your classroom practice?

Here is your opportunity to express your theoretical understanding of teaching and learning. Your interviewers want to know about your theoretical knowledge and how you relate it to specific classroom activities. Identify the general principles of learning you ascribe to. Connect those principles to some classroom activities. Describe how you plan to adapt specific theories or principles of learning to specific students. Discuss some of the possible consequences of implementing your theories. Explain how you will integrate theory into your practical decision making. Your classroom practice derives from your educational beliefs, and you need to be able to articulate the connections between them. Reread the questions and note topics you would discuss. Use this time, when you are not pressured by the interview setting, to organize your thoughts.

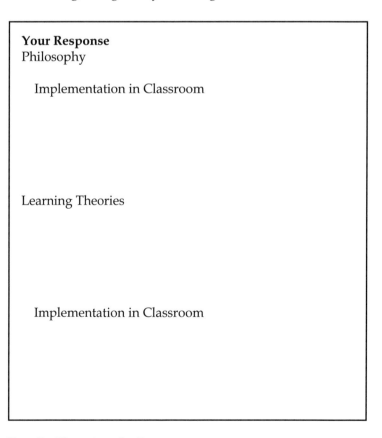

Your Response
Philosophy

Implementation in Classroom

Learning Theories

Implementation in Classroom

PRACTICE ISSUE 3

NOTES NOTES NOTES

SUPPORTING LEARNING

Tell us what makes a classroom supportive of learning.

What are the most important ways a teacher can help students?

Describe your system of classroom management.

Classroom management is fundamental to student learning. It ranges from authoritarian to collaborative, from person to person, and from situation to situation. Your style of classroom management should be consistent with what you believe is conducive to learning. As you reflect, you may want to address such issues as support for the students' academic, emotional, and social growth; organization of interactions or activities in the classroom; and establishment of classroom rules collaboratively by the teacher and the students.

Your Response
What experiences can you relate that convey your concept of classroom organization and its impact on learning?

Relate an experience that connects classroom organization to learning.

PRACTICE ISSUE 4

IMPRESSIONS OF TEACHING

Describe one of the best teachers you observed or recall.

Tell us about a memorable experience from your own history as a student.

School experiences that produce lasting memories frequently are personal rather than academic. The interviewers' request offers you the opportunity to reflect on your wealth of experiences and select a powerful, emotional, learning event. Your recognition of the psychosocial nature of growth and development of your students is being addressed in these requests. Your response will suggest your learning style, your teaching style, and your values, particularly as they might influence your teaching. Remember, your interviewers are seeking to visualize the classroom you will create. They are asking you to help them envision it. In this instance, they ask how your personal reflections on your experiences will guide your classroom practice.

Your Response
Record how you could use this type of question to convey what you believe is excellent teaching.

PRACTICE ISSUE 5

CLASSROOM LESSONS

How would you set up a classroom reading (math, critical thinking) program?

Describe a typical math lesson.

How will your classroom activities address our new curriculum standards?

The interviewers want to know your level of readiness for teaching and your understanding of curriculum, classroom organization, and how children learn. Here is a good opportunity to communicate your knowledge of local, state, or national learning standards; curriculum innovations; and curricular decision making. Reflect on activities that you have developed and implemented based on students' academic needs and the learning standards required in your area to support your response.

Your Response
Note some specific activities and the connections to current curriculum goals.

PRACTICE ISSUE 6

PERSONAL APPROACHES

What do you do <u>in your spare time</u> (to relax)?

What do you hope to be doing <u>in 10 years</u>?

These questions seek information about your personal approach to life and to teaching. You can convey multiple interests, energy, and involvement in your community, as well as your vision of your career as a teacher. Here is an opportunity to disclose the personal interests and activities that may be useful in setting you apart from other candidates. You may also address any qualifications that you had planned to include in this interview but have not yet mentioned.

Be cautious about responding with personal information that should not be included in your evaluation, such as age, marital status, plans for having children, and so on. If personal questions are asked, you face a dilemma. You have a legal right to refuse to answer such questions. You may answer fully, or you can finesse the conversation in another direction. You will see how Kippi handles this when you read her scenario. Consider not only the consequences of your decision, but also the implications about the school if such requests are routinely made.

Your Response
Make a list of topics you might include in your response.

PRACTICE ISSUE 7

YOUR QUESTIONS

What questions do you have for us?

Is there anything we haven't covered that you would like to know?

You have shared much information with us; are there some things that we can share with you?

A typical conclusion to an interview is the offer to the candidate to ask some questions. Here is a triple opportunity: You may ask a direct question about a topic that is important to you, you may pose a question related to one of your strengths that you had not been able to mention, or you may convey your knowledge about the school or district.

You want to communicate your strengths as a knowledgeable educator by asking academically related questions. There will be ample time to ask about benefits, hours, and salary after the school offers you the position and before you accept it. Your questions will suggest your professional priorities.

Your Response
Note some questions that reflect professional concerns.

SUMMING UP

At your interview, you will interpret each question carefully and convey information that both satisfies the interviewer and shows your best qualities. Of course, this is easier said than done. In your interpretation of each practice question, you have focused on issues that are sometimes obscured by different terms and by words that are synonymous or are used synonymously. We presented questions that suggest diverse opinions as well as issues that are controversial or inappropriate. Responding to such requests is difficult, but practice, such as that given in this chapter, helps. Continue to analyze information, identify the issues, and organize your ideas through note taking, which will enable you to respond more comprehensively to typical questions posed in chapter 7.

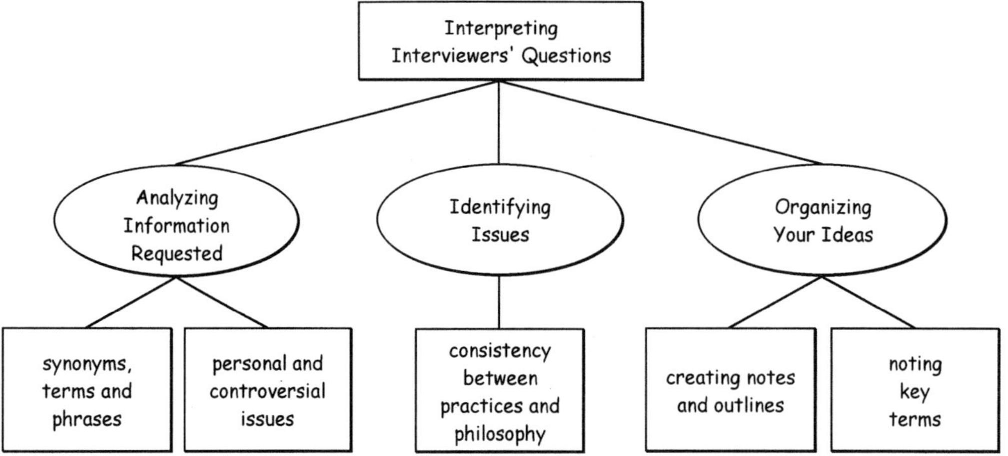

PART D

PREPARING YOURSELF

Communicating your best qualities as a teacher requires skill in verbal expression as well as skill in conveying your confidence through your personal demeanor. You will improve your presentation as you participate in the detailed practice in this section by analyzing interview questions, developing responses that reflect your strengths and suitability for a particular teacher opening, and articulating your confidence. Marcy interacts with several principals with different perspectives on literacy instruction. This setting enables us to identify her knowledge and beliefs as reflected in the practice she is advocating. All of these activities are essential in preparing for your interviews.

SCENARIO

Marcy Ramos

A District-Based, Second Interview With Several Principals

Candidate:	Marcy Ramos	
Interviewers:	Ed Ballin	Principal, Lakeview Middle School
	Gloria Terno	Principal, Juno Primary School
	Terry Nentes	Principal, Parkview Elementary
	Lisa Linder	Principal, Marra Elementary School

Marcy responded to an advertisement listing five openings in the Lakeview School District. From a paper screening of 150 résumés, 50 candidates were selected for first-level interviews with individual principals. After these interviews, the 12 successful candidates were interviewed by the team to further narrow the pool. Marcy is 1 of the 12.

WHO IS MARCY?

Marcy is quite comfortable as she prepares for her interview at Lakeview because it reminds her of the suburban town in which she grew up. Children progress from the schools in winter to the town pool in summer, and on to neighboring day camps until school starts again in September. Most go on to college and, like Marcy, they find employment during their undergraduate summers in their own or nearby communities.

In a way Marcy has been preparing her whole life for this moment, and many of her experiences—camp, summer tutoring, and a natural inclination toward helping and being with people—have brought her to this room.

She comes directly from a prestigious state university where she majored in English and minored in education. She is from a large, education-oriented family; two of her older sisters are also teachers. Marcy believes she was "born" to be a teacher and is eager to proceed with the next step in the process—landing the job.

She is convinced, especially after her first interview with Ed Ballin, Principal of Lakeview Middle School, that she is being asked back because of her summer school tutoring experiences. Let's listen in on her second interview at the Lakeview School District. After brief introductions of all those sitting at the table, Marcy's interviewers are ready to discuss substantive issues.

THE INTERVIEW

Terry Nentes: Marcy, your résumé states that you worked summers throughout college, preparing fifth, sixth, and seventh graders to pass courses they failed during the school year. What academic subjects did you cover?

Marcy: I worked for 3 years in that program. The first two summers I did reading, writing, and spelling. We read books and talked about them in the class and we wrote stories. During the third summer, I tutored mathematics. I enjoyed working with the struggling learners and I enjoyed learning some things all over again, especially math. It was like going back to basics for myself as well as for the students. I learned about going back to the beginning with a learner who is having difficulty with the material. [1]

KEEP IN MIND

[1]There was no "tell me about yourself" icebreaker. The Lakeview principals began the interview with a question relating to Marcy's résumé. She took Ms. Nentes's question about academic subjects and turned it into a "tell me about yourself" response regarding her experiences.

(continued)

Ed Ballin: To follow up on what Ms. Nentes was saying, you were dealing with a small group of fifth, sixth, seventh, and eighth graders in a summer school setting. How do you think you'd manage 26 or 27 fourth graders? [2]

NOTES NOTES NOTES

Mr. Ballin, a middle school principal, asks a pointed question that warrants careful thought. What do you think he might be looking for?

Marcy: Oh, I've worked with large groups before and I come from a large family, and I've had lots of experience organizing games for large groups at camp. Why I even helped out in gym classes when I was student teaching. I wore a whistle around my neck and I'm very good at getting their attention. Kids listen to me generally and so management wasn't a problem. You see, if you keep them involved and physically active, then you don't have trouble. If you give me the opportunity, I could demonstrate how I handle large groups. [3]

Gloria Terno: Marcy, it certainly sounds as if you know how to handle large groups in a summer camp setting, but I'd like to talk to you about the fourth-grade academic program. You talked about reading, writing, and spelling in summer school. What kind of literacy program would you have in your room if we offered you the fourth-grade position?

Marcy: Well, Ms. Terno, I like fourth grade and it interests me particularly because I have two nieces who are in that grade and we're always talking about the books they're reading. I get such different insights about the reactions of young people that obviously I didn't have when reading as a child.

KEEP IN MIND

Marcy talked about going back to the beginning with struggling learners. Notice how she turned the word *failed* in Ms. Nentes's question into *struggling learner* in her answer. She suggests that we all learn in different ways and she will be attuned to her students' learning styles, thus sharing a key tenet of her teaching and learning philosophy. She hinted about her weakness in math, but provided a sense that she's ready to learn and that she will be a lifelong learner.

[2]Mr. Ballin wants to know Marcy's ideas and strategies for classroom management. As a middle school principal, he's interested in knowing if she can discipline and control her students and he wants to see if she has a philosophy about curriculum and teaching in relation to large-group and small-group instruction.

[3]Marcy's response was very brief, omitting any reference to specific strategies she might use. She might want to think about preparing some generic responses so that when she hears the trigger words *manage* or *discipline* in a question, she will be alert to the kind of information being sought.

I think literacy is a combination of reading, writing, listening, speaking, and thinking. My literacy program would have all the materials and strategies that would further those aspects of the language arts. I will read aloud to my students every day no matter what grade I teach. I will stock a classroom library with books that I collected from various sources. I'd ask the principal for books. I'd go to the school library. I'd ask the children to lend some of their books for the year, and I'm developing my own cache of books for my classroom library. I started studying children's literature while taking my education courses and now I own a good number of books that appeal to children of all ages. These books would be used for sustained silent reading, which my students would participate in every day.

We will have book talks about the books they are reading and we'll do this in groups during the reading program. Children will sit in small groups reading the same book and they'll address certain issues that pertain to the reading of the day. I will have prepared a set of key questions covering the pages read by the group for that day. It's a lot of work but I do believe this process makes for a good learning experience and a good reading experience.

For example, let's say some small groups are reading *Bridge to Terabithia* by Katherine Paterson [1977] and they're reading the second chapter. After they have had time to enter their thoughts in their response journals, I'd distribute a sheet suggesting three or four discussion points. A typical sheet might ask the group to discuss two things: the family's attitude toward Jesse's friendship with a girl and the narrator's meaning when talking about what "would become of the relationship."

Reading process is only one part of my literacy program. As you see we'll have response journal writing and sharing. We'll have writer's workshop every day, which starts with the whole group, and it is here that I focus on skills that I noticed were lacking in their early drafts. At this point I would teach skills to the whole group, and then follow up as I go around the room and visit each child individually. [4]

Lisa Linder: You sound convincing when you speak about reading instruction being so individualized, but are you really going

---

KEEP IN MIND

[4]Marcy displayed knowledge of elements of a literacy program and expanded on them by explaining the ways in which the reading process might work. She mentioned teaching skills within her literacy program. She was alert to Ms. Terno's use of the word *literacy* and responded by citing particular books, titles, and authors.

to instruct children in reading with all this book talk? When are they going to learn about reading?

Marcy: When you say "learn about reading," if you're referring to the actual word attack strategies, those fit into the skills instruction part of my reading program, every day. Phonics instruction goes hand in hand with opportunities to identify words in meaningful sentences and stories. For example, with young, emergent readers, when I read them a story such as *Mrs. Wishy Washy* [Cowley, 1999], the "W" is very visible, especially if I'm reading from a big book. Many, but not all, will be able to identify the "W" in the context of the story and many will be able to point to it during our second and third reading of the story. If there are some children who need a little extra time to learn the "W," I will work with them individually and in small groups. The same process is true for older children during a guided reading lesson or even a read-aloud session. As we read, I'll model for them the ideas I'm having and the questions I'm asking myself. We'll discuss strategies for bringing meaning to the print, for recognizing words, and for understanding the words on the page. Reading instruction will take place often in the context of whatever we're working with and will carry over to science reading, social studies reading, and even math reading. [5]

Gloria Terno: Yes, but what kind of "teaching" of reading will you do? When will you actually teach them about reading?

Marcy: Yes, Ms. Terno, you're pointing out something very important that I've learned about teaching reading. Guided reading is the best time in the program to teach reading and should occur every day when students are clustered in small groups. This guided reading time will be the time when I'd do most of my teaching about reading.

NOTES NOTES NOTES

Suggest a response to Ms. Linder's question, "When are they going to learn about reading?"

KEEP IN MIND

[5]After talking about her philosophy of learning and her belief that children learn best in small groups, Marcy interpreted Ms. Linder's question, "When are they going to learn about reading?" as reflective of a more structured orientation. Because she "listened" to the wording of the questions, Marcy mentioned teaching phonics within the context of literature and assured her interviewers that indeed she would be addressing reading strategies and word attack skills on a regular basis. She wanted to make sure her interviewers didn't perceive her as "touchy feely." Marcy presented herself as knowledgeable about process, content, children, and ways of learning. She presented a teaching plan that is informed and holistic.

NOTES NOTES NOTES

How would you respond to Ms. Terno's question on guided reading in the upper grades?

Gloria Terno: Yes, but I understand guided reading is used in the lower grades where the teacher explains everything she's doing as a reader. How does this differ in the upper grades?

Marcy: In order to create guided reading groups in the upper grades, I will listen to individuals read and document their reading strategies. Based on this assessment, I'll know where they need help and I'll choose appropriate books for us to read and discuss together.

During the last part of my student teaching, I had the opportunity to try this out. I worked with the same group of fifth graders every day. The school subscribed to one publisher for all their language arts materials and so we worked with a literature anthology. We frequently talked about the story before we read it, established what everybody already knew, and then read the story silently before we talked about the meaning we got from the reading. This kind of lesson is powerful because it allows children to share their learning with the group and sometimes they surprise themselves with how much they know. These small groups allow for individualizing skills instruction, and I believe that skills are retained longer when they are taught as needed and reinforced on an individual basis. [6]

Gloria Terno: Well, Marcy, the reading program you describe certainly sounds interesting. As we explained, this was the second go-round in the interview process. If we call you back it will be for a demonstration lesson and a writing sample. We'll be in touch with more particulars. Again, thank you.

What strengths did Marcy display that would encourage the interview team to call her back?

KEEP IN MIND

[6]Marcy related her student teaching experience working with an anthology and small groups, assuring her interviewers that she would encourage students to explore the story, extend the story, and talk about the story. She addressed the issue of instruction, communicating her philosophy that strategies are learned best and retained longer when targeted and taught as needed. Marcy pointed out her belief that all children do not learn at the same rate or in the same way and that her classroom will accommodate many types of learners. She's listening for cues and "hearing" the agenda of her interviewers and addressing their beliefs in relation to her philosophy.

SUMMING UP

Looking back at her interview, Marcy was able to recall some positive aspects in her performance and to identify some parts that she will modify for future interviews. Marcy integrated her philosophy about teaching the struggling learner and the fact that she herself will always be learning. She presented herself as a willing and knowledgeable candidate, eager to contribute to the school community. She injected her ideas about teaching and learning into her responses about tutoring.

Overall, she was pleased with the way she answered many of the questions and hoped she would be called again by the district. There were many reasons Marcy might be called back for a demonstration lesson and writing sample. Her demeanor is positive and professional. She's thoughtful, she's involved, and she knows children. She keeps current with their literature and is very much aware of children's interests and styles. She seems quite resourceful in recognizing and acquiring whatever is needed for her students. She appears organized and it seems as if she'll be able to manage a classroom full of youngsters. Perhaps she'll get the job. She believes that she communicated her strengths as shown in her mnemonic, WORKS:

W – Well-managed classroom
O – Organized
R – Responsive to children
K – Knowledgeable
S – Summer tutoring

CHAPTER 7 RESPONDING AT INTERVIEWS

AT A GLANCE

In this chapter we continue to explore your major responsibilities at the interview:

- Listen to questions.
- Convey your qualifications.
- Learn about the school.

The process includes *sample spontaneous responses* and *sample thoughtful responses*. Starting with extensive scaffolding, there is a gradual reduction of suggestions and support. In a cyclical process with eight questions, you will build on the skills practiced in chapter 6 and increase your ease in developing your own responses.

NOTES NOTES NOTES

Because you have little or no control over the questions you are asked in an interview, you must prepare for many possibilities. This chapter offers a systematic process for analyzing questions and developing responses.

As you practice responding to questions, you are encouraged to develop clear, concise statements in several domains: your knowledge about teaching and learning, your experiences, and your beliefs. Your answers will reflect your unique qualities. As a candidate for a position, you have three major responsibilities:

1. To *listen* to the questions. Listening carefully helps you to analyze, identify, and organize the issues.

2. To *convey* your qualifications. Look for opportunities to communicate your strongest qualities. Expect that any topic you mention may result in a follow-up inquiry requiring you to provide greater detail.

3. To *learn* about the school. Listen and observe carefully to gather information and insights about the school.

In the following guided practice, we present eight predictable requests:

- Tell us about yourself.
- What is your philosophy of education?
- Describe your system of classroom management.
- How will you evaluate the progress of your students?
- Tell us about some professional literature that you have read lately.
- How will you adjust your instruction for special-needs children in your classroom?
- How will you address the learning needs of English language learners or bilingual students?
- How will technology be part of your teaching?

We will guide you through reviewing, critiquing, and developing your own thoughtful and professional responses. We provide extensive support initially and encourage your gradual independence as you develop responses to these typical issues.

A Spontaneous Response

I just completed my teacher education program at __________ College. I always wanted to be a teacher and used to play teacher when I was a child. My experiences in student teaching proved that I made the right decision. I student taught in Grades 3 and 5 and loved it. The kids loved me and we had fun every day. I like sports and I like to travel.

This answer conveys personal enjoyment, teacher satisfaction, and a superficial emphasis on fun. It misses opportunities to mention positive personal characteristics and experiences.

Your Spontaneous Response

Try your hand at answering this typical interview request: "Tell us about yourself." Include connections between your interests and benefits to your students.

A Thoughtful Response

I just completed my teacher education program at ________ College. I always liked children and volunteered and worked in child care, sports, and tutoring situations while I was a student. Each experience taught me more about how varied and wonderful children are and how much I would have to learn to be an effective teacher. I recall the varied responses from my tutoring group when I played unfamiliar music on the piano for them. I could see a connection with music and literacy. I studied very hard in my teacher education program and participated fully in my student teacher placements. I was able to develop wonderful communication with my cooperating teachers. I was part of their planning activities, and I assumed more and more responsibility until I was able to plan and develop integrated units and implement them as a solo teacher.

This response relates how the candidate rationally tested a personal inclination toward teaching. He chose volunteer and student employment that involved helping children. The candidate demonstrated an understanding of a personal learning process and mentioned an additional skill (piano playing). He clearly values communication among teachers and stresses experience in planning.

Your Thoughtful Response

Revise your response to emphasize your qualities that will be beneficial to students.

Based on your Thoughtful Response, choose three adjectives that describe you as a teacher.

WHAT IS YOUR PHILOSOPHY OF EDUCATION?

A Spontaneous Response
My philosophy of education is to make education fun and help children learn as much as they can. I think each child should get along with others. Students should learn the basic skills and be able to get a job and be self-sufficient.

The candidate is missing opportunities to talk about any theoretical knowledge learned in the teacher education program. Specific understandings about children and child development are noticeably missing.

Why may an interviewer value theoretical or philosophical statements?

Your Spontaneous Response
Identify some theoretical statements you might offer when asked this question.

A Thoughtful Response
My philosophy of education will be implemented in my classroom, centering on respecting students as individuals. I believe students must be listened to and encouraged to engage fully in all the activities in their classrooms. They will then grow into respecting themselves and others. They will learn by listening, speaking, reading, and writing.

Schools must provide structure enough to enhance social living, creativity, and personal growth. I like Bruner's idea of scaffolding using structure to provide assistance and direction until the students take responsibility for their learning. I believe children grow through hard work and challenging tasks when these tasks are filled with meaning, understanding, and increased responsibility. By listening to our students and getting to know them, we can connect to their lives and interests. We need to provide quality tasks, support, encouragement, and guidance so students can achieve high quality; this is documented in the writings of _________ and ___________.

I believe that children are our future, our neighbors, and our children's neighbors; they are citizens of the world-to-be on whom we will depend. A great philosopher stated that what each parent wants for his or her own child, the community must want for all its children.

This response uses formal educational terminology. The references to classroom practice include:

- Acknowledging differences.
- Learning from personal experiences.
- Understanding the individual student.
- Providing organization and structure.
- Preparing students for participation in the larger society.

It conveys formal learning and theoretical knowledge. Referring to a philosopher or theory elevates the answer above activities that are primarily "fun." The combination of philosophy and methodology provides the picture of a knowledgeable teacher who makes informed decisions about classroom practice.

Your Thoughtful Response
Evaluate and revise your response to address broad philosophical concepts. Make your response precise, specific, and relevant to classroom practice.

DESCRIBE YOUR SYSTEM OF CLASSROOM MANAGEMENT

A Spontaneous Response
I think classroom management is the most important part of being a teacher. If you don't have good classroom management, you cannot accomplish anything. I want my students to accomplish a lot in my classroom, so I will establish my system of classroom rules on the first day. I will make it very clear and explicit what the rules are and what the consequences are for breaking the rules. It will take some weeks before the behavior I expect becomes routine, but I will be consistent and fair. I have been told that not much learning can take place while you are establishing the rules of the class, but the learning will come later.

This response stresses teacher control. The repeated "I" emphasizes a one-directional system. There is no indication that this candidate is likely to consider the students' characteristics when administering or modifying a management system. There are no specific examples of how the management would operate, nor is there any connection between management and instruction.

Your Spontaneous Response
Develop a response that clearly shows your understanding of students, of classrooms, and of learning. Describe how you organized a specific teaching activity including:

- Seating.
- Materials.
- Movement of students.

A Thoughtful Response

Classroom management is vitally important in a classroom. I hope my students will be orderly and respectful and be able to work individually and in groups. I know such an environment doesn't happen automatically. Students must sense that they are sharing in it from the beginning. They need to be involved in developing, modifying, and enforcing the rules and consequences. We will need quiet times, work-talk times, and chat times. When learners are thoroughly engaged in meaningful activities, disruptive behavior is minimized. A well-organized room and good planning reduce that idle transition time that invites disruptive behaviors.

I recently taught an integrated unit on ancient cultures. When we were researching the kingdoms of Egypt, each of four groups researched a different kingdom, using different books, and preparing different kinds of reports. The time-on-task was wonderful. Sometimes the noise level rose, but each student was talking about the project, comparing notes, and sharing new and fascinating information. My preparation was extensive, but it was worth it. There were few discipline problems, very little lost time, materials were easily available, and directions were clear. The students worked hard, collaborated on decisions, and enjoyed each part of the project, and so did I.

Compare the categories in your spontaneous response to those in the simulated thoughtful response.

The candidate moved from general principles of organization and participation, referring to students, learners, groups, and working individually. The response focused on student activity and outcomes. Describing a personally developed and implemented project substantiates that this is a tried system.

Your Thoughtful Response
Improve your response by adding brief examples and by mentioning the classroom atmosphere that you think is important.

HOW WILL YOU EVALUATE THE PROGRESS OF YOUR STUDENTS?

Using terms other than "evaluate" and "progress," how will you convey your ideas and satisfy the interviewer?

A Spontaneous Response
I think grades are necessary. We are moving toward national tests and we need to let parents and students know how the scores compare to others in this country. Grades help students focus on what they should do to acquire an education. It motivates them to study.

The candidate interpreted the word *evaluate* as meaning teacher grading, although the question actually referred to student progress. The response should have the same emphasis as the question; that is, progress of the students in the classroom. National tests may be one way of evaluating progress, but these tests may have little connection with the curriculum. We still need to hear specific strategies for evaluating the impact of this candidate's instruction on student progress.

Your Spontaneous Response

A Thoughtful Response

Whenever my students say or do something, I always evaluate them. I think teaching any lesson involves constant assessment that is twofold—teacher driven and learner driven. Learners should be involved in their own assessment and thus their own grades. I will establish a variety of assessment tools, and I'll make sure that each student has a role in the assessment process. I will help students to develop criteria for assessing their own learning. For example, I will use portfolios to accumulate their writing and have them reflect on the effectiveness of their stories. In this way, the students' awareness of responsibility for learning is made clear. This motivates learners and helps them develop independence.

The state requires many tests. Colleges use standardized tests for admission and the country is moving toward national tests and national standards. So we can't ignore standardized tests and normed grades, but I hope to have my students understand assessment and participate in it.

The emphasis in this response mirrors the emphasis in the question: the students. The candidate addresses this question from a general stance and with reference to specific practices. This candidate volunteered extra information about testing trends and practices, which shows that she keeps up with professional information.

What have you learned about the school from this question?

Your Thoughtful Response
Rethink your response to make it consistent with your philosophy and rewrite it here.

NOTES NOTES NOTES

TELL US ABOUT SOME PROFESSIONAL LITERATURE THAT YOU HAVE READ LATELY

A Spontaneous Response
My teacher education program was very intensive, and I was given many reading assignments. I was a conscientious student and had little time for outside activities. Some of the texts I read for my courses include a textbook on foundations of education and a book about teaching reading.

The reference to reading assignments probably reflects most candidates' experiences. The response might imply that the candidate struggled with the requirements and had no time to do more than the minimum required. The candidate interprets the question to refer to independent reading beyond the class assignments, although the question does not exclude course readings. The vague references to textbooks, without author or title, suggest a less than attentive student.

Your Spontaneous Response
Develop a response that conveys your knowledge of professional literature:

- Include the authors and titles of the books.
- Mention professional periodicals and newspapers.

A Thoughtful Response

Although my teacher education program was very intensive and the reading assignments were extensive, I had the opportunity to read some recommended journals my teachers have referred to frequently. I found _________ and _________ very useful because _________. Some of the authors I read for my courses who particularly interested me include _________ and _________. I plan to reread some of those selections again and locate some of their other writings. An article I read in _______________ has caused me to rethink how I will organize my literacy program.

What does this response convey about the candidate's balance between free time and professional development?

This response provides a view of a literate person. It shows confidence and the ability to go beyond the minimum assignments. The emphasis on independent learning suggests that this candidate will not become stale and rigid as the world changes. A word of caution: Be sure that this answer (and every answer) is absolutely true. Remember, the interviewer may inquire further about any item you mention.

Your Thoughtful Response
Review your first response in light of the two preceding analyses and revise it to convey additional professionalism.

We list three additional questions posed frequently at interviews. We encourage you to work these through by bulleting ideas spontaneously before you draft a thoughtful narrative response. Use the critical analysis skills you developed in this chapter to enhance your responses.

HOW WILL YOU ADJUST YOUR INSTRUCTION FOR SPECIAL-NEEDS CHILDREN IN YOUR CLASSROOM?

Your Spontaneous Response

Your Thoughtful Response

HOW WILL YOU ADDRESS THE LEARNING NEEDS OF ENGLISH LANGUAGE LEARNERS OR BILINGUAL STUDENTS?

NOTES NOTES NOTES

Your Spontaneous Response

What inferences do you make about the values of your interviewers and the school based on the questions asked?

Your Thoughtful Response

HOW WILL COMPUTER TECHNOLOGY BE PART OF YOUR TEACHING?

NOTES NOTES NOTES

Your Spontaneous Response

How have your experiences with computer software, video disk, and the Internet enhanced your response?

Your Thoughtful Response

SUMMING UP

The practice you have just engaged in helped you to rethink and organize the knowledge you have accumulated in many settings: your teacher education classes, your field experiences, and your life experiences. By reviewing, critiquing, and reflecting on questions and sample responses, you rehearsed the thinking process that will enable you to develop professional responses for yourself. You may want to revisit these steps as you practice with other questions. Each practice increases your awareness of the need to respond accurately, to make connections between the interviewer's interest and your qualifications, and to develop insights into the school philosophy and style.

Remember the three focal points you need to address in each interview:

1. **Listen to the questions.** Analyze the information requested and organize your ideas.

2. **Convey your qualifications.** Look for opportunities to communicate your strongest qualities.

3. **Learn about the school.** Listen and observe carefully to gather information and insights about the school.

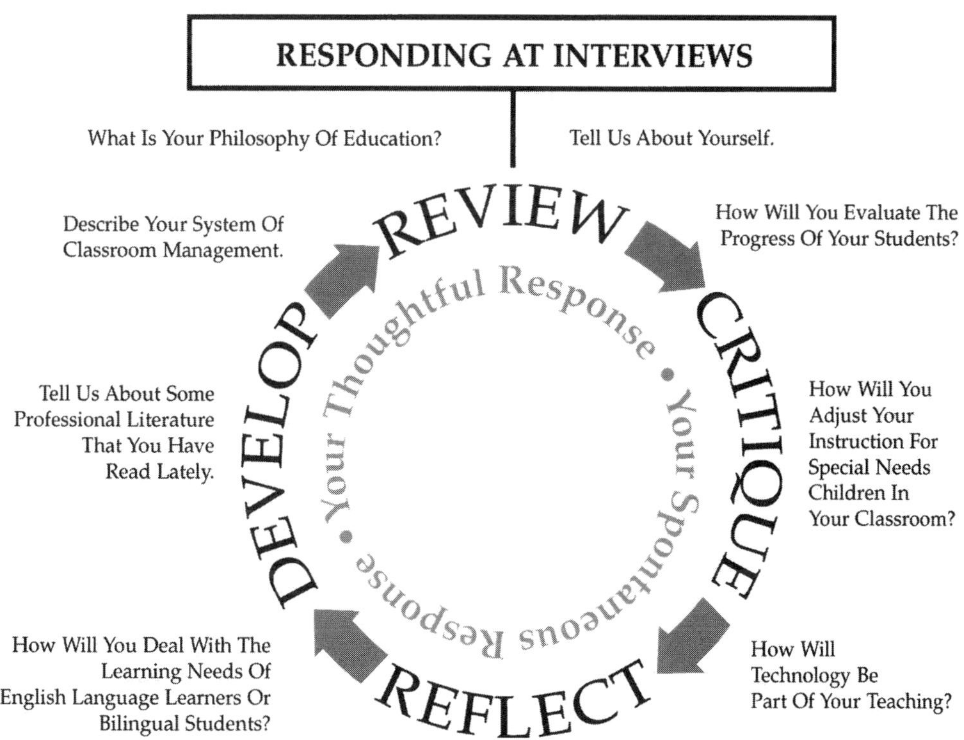

CHAPTER 8 CRITIQUING TYPICAL RESPONSES

AT A GLANCE

Together we will critique unedited responses of teacher interns who spontaneously answered questions most frequently asked at interviews:

- Why should our school hire you?
- What special characteristics do you bring to a school, to a classroom, to students?

Considering three aspects of responding—examining, analyzing, and developing responses—we sharpen the focus of your preparation.

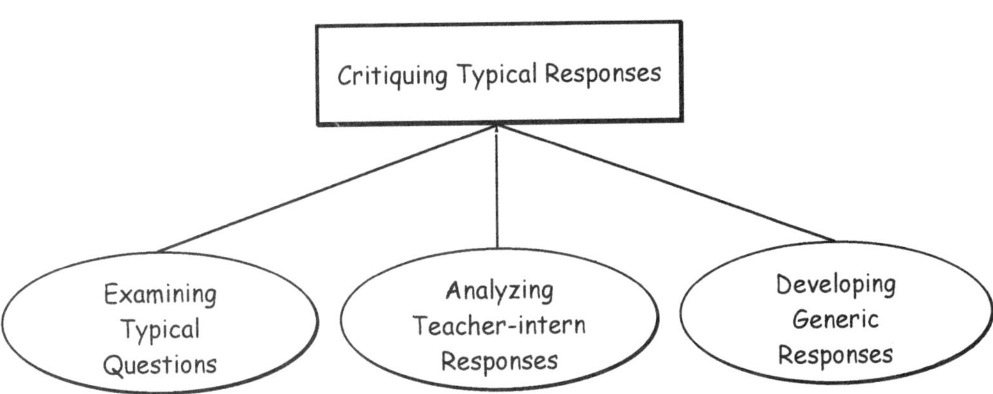

As a candidate for a teaching position, you are not usually able to hear others' responses to the questions often asked at interviews. We did the next best thing. We asked 40 teacher interns (we use the terms *teacher intern* and *candidate* interchangeably) to respond spontaneously to two frequently asked questions. It is useful to study some of these unedited responses as a way to clarify the issues that are of greatest import to you and eavesdrop on what others might be saying. We devote this chapter to helping you analyze responses to each question and develop your own answers.

Highlighting the competitive nature of the hiring process, interviewers frequently pose this first question or include it in the application questionnaire.

WHY SHOULD OUR SCHOOL HIRE YOU?

This question appeared in both Steve's and Jennifer's interviews. We think it would be useful for you to prepare a generic response for the question before we discuss it further. We admit that this is difficult without having a particular school in mind; you cannot shape your response to the unique qualities of that setting. It may be that you will know little about the school in which you are interviewing, in that case a generic response will be useful. Knowledge of the school may facilitate your response, but developing generic responses will help you in several ways: identify your special qualities, clarify your understanding of teaching, and practice your communication techniques in an interview. Take the time now to list some specific qualities that you can offer a school.

What unique qualities could you discuss in answer to the question, "Why should our school hire you?"

Let's look at five actual responses gathered from the interns and note the issues addressed in each.

- I feel that my commitment to improving the quality of urban education, as well as my proven dedication to the students I serve, make me an excellent candidate for a teaching position in your school.
- I am dedicated to what teaching is all about, which to me is about making a difference in a child's life. I am a team player and love being part of a staff. I am determined to be an excellent teacher.
- I have experience teaching. I am willing to make a commitment to education and prepare children to be healthy, productive citizens. I am willing to constantly increase my knowledge of current methods in teaching and improve my abilities to be an effective teacher. I care about children.
- Your district should hire me because I bring to the classroom a sense of authority while still being approachable.

My objective is to offer students a safe, hands-on learning environment while giving them a foundation by which to become productive members of our pluralistic society. I will never forget my motto that "All children can succeed."

- I plan to bring my knowledge of literature and government and politics (my college majors) into the classroom. I have already begun to do this with my class, and I have seen positive effects. I would also like to bring art into activities. More than ever, arts are needed in our schools, and I'd like to be a part of bringing it into our schools.

List some qualities the candidates addressed in response to the question.

Qualities:

We have spent much time looking over the interns' responses and were able to identify many qualities and different styles of response. Now we suggest that you compare your list with ours.

Qualities

Although each response reflects unique priorities, there are three qualities that are frequently mentioned, namely:

- *Dedication to students* (make a difference in a child's life; prepare children to be healthy, productive citizens; care about children; approachable; offer a safe, hands-on learning environment; "All children can succeed").
- *Dedication to the profession* (determined to be an excellent teacher; constantly increase my knowledge and improve my abilities).
- *Experience* (sense of authority; knowledge of literature and government and politics; bring art into activities).

We can infer from this analysis that interns believe that dedication to students and the profession and personal experience are important qualities to bring to a school. These qualities are also valued by schools. Two respondents included unique concerns, thereby distinguishing themselves from the others being interviewed:

- *Commitment to improving urban education.*
- *Ability to work as a team member.*

Each individual's sense of responsibility as a teacher is becoming clear. The personal qualities that will distinguish one classroom from another and one colleague from another become apparent in the comments. Some of the issues that are addressed in these comments may be organized topically, for example:

- *Goal orientation* (team player, eager to learn, excellent teacher, making a difference).
- *Content knowledge* (literature, government, politics).
- *Curricular activities* (art).
- *Classroom organization* (authority).
- *Self-promotion* (commitment, dedication, and enthusiasm).
- *Self-confidence* (ability to teach in the district).

While presenting issues that are important to them, the teacher interns implicitly indicated important characteristics of their personal style. One repeated the question, perhaps as a stall to gather ideas, perhaps as a way to confirm that the question heard is the one that was offered, or perhaps as a way to frame the response. It is not unusual for candidates to misconstrue or mishear at least one interview question. On the other hand, a candidate may intentionally redirect the focus of a question, as you will see in Kippi's scenario. All of these teacher interns heard the question accurately and responded to it.

Their responses were brief, suggesting a desire to get on to the next question rather than to take the opportunity to elaborate on some of their unique qualities. Sometimes candidates believe that it is their responsibility to provide brief, to-the-point responses. The candidate may believe that if the interviewer wants additional information, there will be a follow-up question. Other candidates take the opportunity when they have the floor to expand on their responses, offering examples of their experiences as a way to communicate their strengths. These candidates expect that if the interviewers would prefer to go on to another topic, they would not hesitate to interrupt. On the other hand, they recognize that when they have the opportunity to explain their ideas, they do it to their advantage. This strategy is particularly important in the case of structured interviews discussed in chapter 5.

The candidates conveyed a sense of commitment, dedication, and enthusiasm by explicitly using these specific words and by the eagerness in their responses. They exhibited a clear desire to make a good impression and to be considered in a good light.

Global generalities, however, pervade the responses offered by these candidates. We do not really get to know most of them from the responses offered. Only once does a candidate advance an academic background as a resource for the curriculum. Each suggests a level of confidence in being selected as the teacher for the district's opening, and that is a positive stance. If candidates justify confidence by relating experiences, their answers become more compelling.

Try your hand at a carefully developed response to the question, "Why should our school hire you?"

Perhaps you have analyzed these responses through a different lens. We now encourage you to synthesize our comments with your own, reflect on the similarities and differences, and then revise your response to the question under review. Remember that this question is an opportunity to emphasize *your unique talents* and to have the district rank you as the first choice. Develop a carefully considered response that is both truthful and accurate about your perceptions of yourself as a teacher.

Now that we've looked at one predictable question through numerous lenses, we're ready to consider another question.

NOTES NOTES NOTES

WHAT SPECIAL CHARACTERISTICS DO YOU BRING TO A SCHOOL, TO A CLASSROOM, AND TO STUDENTS?

It is likely, with this question, that your interviewers are seeking a match of your qualities with their needs. We begin this segment by expanding your interaction with the text. First we ask you to provide a spontaneous response. Next we present unedited teacher intern responses. Later we ask you to analyze the responses so that you may better understand multiple interpretations of one question. Finally, we present five additional responses and ask you to determine the strengths and limitations of each. The process will further help you to develop a strong personal response to use at your interviews.

We suggest you take time now to write some preliminary thoughts as a generic response to this frequently posed question.

Following are five responses gathered from teacher interns who addressed this question. Consider the issues the interns thought were important.

- I am committed to serving the emotional and educational needs of diverse student populations. I want to encourage my students to see that they are valuable people with valuable points of view and that they matter.
- I want to be the best teacher I can be and I want my students to be the best they can be. Most important is my commitment to education. I want to see that all students who come into my room recognize the importance of learning.
- I bring enthusiasm, excitement, and engagement to all subjects and routines. I have great ideas for a classroom.
- I am cheerful and upbeat even on my worst days. I try to be positive at all times. I am very good at finding the strong points in students. I have a lot of love to give and knowledge I would like to share.
- Each morning I bring a renewed excitement to class instead of remembering a bad moment or lesson that occurred the day before. I also express great expectations for each and every child, no matter what their math or reading level. I have great faith that each child has great ability and I try to express to all children that they are very capable of good work.

Identify issues addressed in the preceding answers.

Issues:

The teacher interns cite special characteristics their interviewers can expect to see if the district hires them. Many of the responses give similar information and are fairly upbeat (e.g., "I have great ideas"). They are enthusiastic, excited, positive, and cheerful. They do, however, overlook some important dimensions in addressing such a question.

What special characteristics will you bring to a school, to a classroom, and to students? This question allows candidates to provide information about their educational and personal background, linking with it specific ways their uniqueness can be transferred to the classroom and to student learning. In reading the responses, did you notice the absence of any important information? Was equal value given to the cognitive and affective areas of teaching and learning?

The teacher interns are eager to talk about the willingness, faith, and enthusiasm they will bring to the classroom. However, they give very few examples of how these traits will be translated to the classroom and to their students. We do not hear how these teachers worked with students to help them to become the best that they can be. Where are the examples of successes they have had? It is refreshing to be exposed to such uplifting aspirations, and we know that the affective domain is a necessary component of teaching. We also know, however, that there are content and curriculum issues that need to be discussed when talking about school and students. Not only enthusiasm, but also skills and knowledge of teaching and learning, are necessary.

The next section consists of five additional teacher intern responses to this question. You will benefit from analyzing each individually.

Identify some classroom activities relevant to these special characteristics.

Explain how this candidate's attitude would be useful in a classroom.

- I am told by many that I am a driven person. I think this is the characteristic that will make me a successful teacher. When I am in a classroom, my goal is to bring every child to a higher level of understanding. Knowing the children helps me to know what will and will not work, what to say and what not to say, how to encourage, and how to discipline. My determination is my strength, but my desire to get to know each child is my special characteristic.
- Having worked in the "business" world, I feel I have learned how to roll with the punches. I always try to get what I need without ruffling feathers. To the classroom I bring my creative nature to create a bright, happy, learning environment. To my students, I bring respect and understanding. In my past experiences with children, sometimes getting through to them is just a matter of letting them know you really care. I have learned how to foster this type of relationship while maintaining my role as adult, teacher, and role model.
- I bring my dignity. I am proud of my accomplishments and I take my work seriously. We are here to make men and women and I am comfortable with myself as a professional, an adult, and a role model. I insist on politeness, respect, and fairness in my classroom and in my personal life. My unique background encompasses music, visual arts, performing arts, writing, publishing, promotion, marketing, clerical work, management, computing, design, philosophy, and so on, and a unique set of talents including

singing, songwriting, painting, orating, and performance. I bring a sense of humor and openness, a sense of wonder, a sense of urgency.

- I have found that I am an exciting person when it comes to teaching. I really enjoy the time when students and I are doing a lesson and I can be myself—a fun, energetic, and enthusiastic person. I love to see the children get into what we are doing and see that the lessons are more fun and interesting. A true compliment to a lesson is when a student walks away thinking that we were playing a game rather than having a lesson. I am creative and this helps to make lessons more interesting. I am addicted to the Internet and its endless resources for graphics, lessons, and ideas.
- My easygoing personality allows me to communicate with all personality types. I adjust well to new settings. I like to involve myself and assist where I can. For example, I would be able to organize or participate in after-school programs where students help to create a spirit of community, decorating hallway walls, or planning a craft fair. The classroom should be a reflection of the students' work. The teacher must be highly organized, creative, and consistent. My creative nature allows me to foster this kind of environment with a community feeling within the classrooms, helping students to work together. I am intuitive. I believe each student is unique and brings a unique set of circumstances into the classroom. My intuitive nature makes it easy for me to get to know each student as an individual. Every day they will write in their journals and I will write back in an ongoing dialog. I will use the knowledge I gain about their personalities to formulate future lesson plans. By including their personal interests into a lesson, students remain engaged and on task.

What information would you add to make this a more comprehensive response?

List your strengths in each of the following:

School

Classroom

Students

As we reflect on all the teacher intern responses, we note their obvious strengths; we sense their enthusiasm and eagerness. They were delighted to list their personal characteristics, seeing themselves as determined and driven human beings. They are organized, talented, and respectful. Some seemed to list everything they ever did in their lifetime. Although they have definite ideas about what they will bring to their classrooms, very few linked their unique qualities to the curriculum. Rarely did they give concrete examples of the ways they will transfer their unique qualities to the school and the classroom. Only one included a classroom activity citing dialog journals as a way to get to know students.

Identify how you will use these strengths to enhance your teaching.

Relate the classroom applications to your philosophy of teaching and learning.

These are important factors to consider as you develop your generic response to the question, "What special characteristics do you bring to a school, a classroom, and to students?" First review your strengths. Second, identify how you will use these strengths to enhance your teaching. Third, relate these applications to your philosophy of teaching and learning. Finally, draft your response.

NOTES NOTES NOTES

If you were on the interview committee would you be impressed with your response? Your interview is an opportunity for you to cite your enthusiasm for teaching, your strengths, and your ideas for your classroom. Help your interviewers to visualize you as a teacher. If you help them to envision you as a member of their school community, you will increase your chances that they will seriously consider you for the position.

SUMMING UP

You have examined a variety of typical questions, you have analyzed responses offered by teacher interns, and you have been asked to improve on them. You have practiced developing your own generic responses to a few frequently posed questions you are likely to experience in your own interviews. We hope these experiences are increasing your confidence.

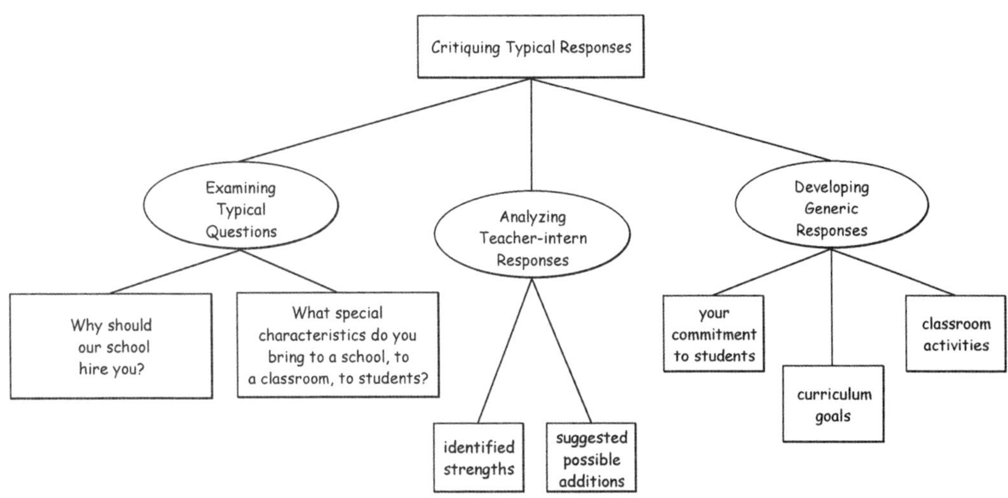

CHAPTER 9

COMMUNICATING YOUR CONFIDENCE: PRACTICE MAKES PERFECT

AT A GLANCE

Practice in projecting professionalism is the theme of this chapter.

We focus on strategies for:

- Communicating your professional strengths.
- Creating a professional presence.

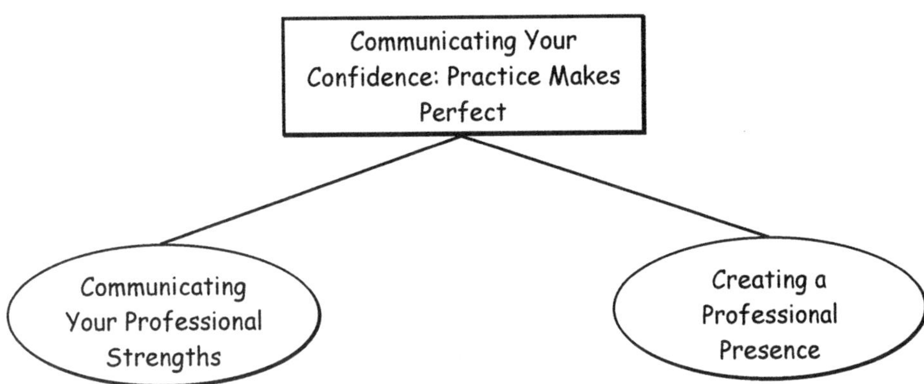

NOTES NOTES NOTES

Projecting your confidence and professionalism in an interview requires systematic practice. In previous chapters you have practiced responding to questions and envisioning the contexts in which you will be interviewed. Your practice addressed the content-oriented elements of the interview process.

You will now focus on your style of presentation, your appearance, your nutrition, and your travel arrangements in preparation for the big day. You will begin to develop strategies to help you remember key points, a mnemonic perhaps. Your interview, however, cannot be staged as if you are performing a script. Use this practice to promote your ability to think on your feet just as you will when you are teaching. As you prepare, you will practice two visible dimensions of interviewing: communicating your professional strengths and creating a professional presence.

COMMUNICATING YOUR PROFESSIONAL STRENGTHS

You will communicate your strengths while you are responding to the inquiries of your interviewers in two ways: what you say and how you say it. Developing generic responses, as you have been doing, will increase your confidence and reduce your stress.

What you say will communicate the depth of your knowledge, experiences, and expertise for the position. Knowing what you want to convey might include planning key anecdotes to include in your responses. Have a plan and work your plan.

- Identify your strongest qualifications and unique experiences.
- Use information from your research of the district to connect your particular strengths with their special concerns.
- Respond to each question directly, clearly, and truthfully.
- As you rehearse, pay careful attention to the content of the questions.

If your research has revealed that the school has few material resources, show how you are creative in this context. If the school has recently reconfigured its literacy program, be ready to connect your experiences teaching writing, for example, to their new program. Communicating your unique qualities, how you will fit in, and what you can offer will set you apart from other candidates. Two useful tools to help you at the interview are your portfolio and your personal reminders.

Compiling a *professional portfolio* is required in many teacher education programs. If you have a portfolio you will certainly want to bring it to the interview. It is a powerful tool to document your strengths in many activities, including these:

- Lesson plans.
- Integrated units.
- Student activities and projects.
- Evaluation instruments.
- Photographs of students at work.
- Samples of student work with brief statements that succinctly convey your purposes and practices.

We've all been told that one picture is worth a thousand words. Make your portfolio more than a simple scrapbook of good memories and successful activities. It should reveal your understanding of professional issues. The educational significance should leap off each page. Visuals and succinct captions can convey your strengths at a glance and are easy to share at an interview. You should identify potential opportunities to use it to your best advantage.

When exactly should you refer to it? If your interviewers ask about reading, for example, be prepared to explain why you organized reading instruction in small groups and support this by directing their attention to the segment of your portfolio that documents your statements. Or, in referring to your lesson plan integrating science and social studies, support your response using that section of the portfolio. The intent is to use your portfolio to strengthen key points you wish to make.

You may consider organizing your portfolio by topics. Strategically place colorful tabs to designate key concepts you want to address, such as your philosophy of learning, thematic teaching, and classroom management. Your portfolio organization can reflect your priorities and your professionalism. A table of contents and tabs, dividers, or colored pages will highlight your understanding as well as your organizational skills. Section headings may include classroom management, integrated learning, social development, and so on, topics that are frequently of great concern to interview committees. See Table 9.1 as an example. With the portfolio divided into such segments, you'll be able to efficiently locate relevant statements and pictures as topics emerge.

Table 9.1 Sample Portfolio Table of Contents

Table of Contents	
Résumé	2
Philosophy of Teaching and Learning	4
Children and Learning	6
Classroom Management	7
Thematic and Integrated Learning	10
Social Development	15
Learning Outside the Walls	18
Personal Adventures	22

You might create a CD-ROM version of your portfolio presentation to leave as a reminder of your strengths. If you do, be sure to note the hardware and software essential for your interviewers' review. This will surely convey your technological sophistication, an asset in most schools.

Mnemonics can be useful memory devices. Personal reminders can help you recall the major points you want to communicate but might overlook in the stress of the interview. Initials or a word may represent important topics you intend to elaborate on. You may recall Felicia's scenario, in which she used the word *educator* as a mnemonic of characteristics she hoped to convey during her interview: **e**ager, **d**edicated, **u**nderstanding, **c**hild oriented, **a**rticulate, **t**houghtful, **o**rganized, and **r**esourceful. Using a word such as *teach* can bring to mind your previously prepared thoughts. Use it as a reminder and a checklist during the interview, for example:

T — Testing
E — Environment
A — Active learning
C — Core curriculum/classroom management
H — Higher order thinking skills

The *T* will remind you of the information you wish to convey about your experiences with testing and evaluation, assessment instruments, and possibly state or national learning standards. The *E* will remind you to talk about your *environment unit*, how you engaged children in cooperative learning groups, or perhaps how you helped special-needs students with their learning. For *A* you may focus your discussion on active learning. For *C* you can talk of your experiences implementing core curriculum and perhaps you can relate this to classroom management. Thinking about *H* is an opportunity for you to recall strategies you used to teach higher order thinking skills.

There are several ways in which you might use your unique mnemonic:

1. Refer to your mnemonic to ensure that you address each issue as you are responding at your interview.

2. You may choose to place your mnemonic on the cover of your portfolio as an integral part of your professional presentation.

3. At the end of the interview you might mentally review your mnemonic, verifying that your responses have covered everything you intended to convey.

What you say, and particularly how you say it, projects your professionalism. Having attained a comfort level with your knowledge, your next challenge is to convey this knowledge and confidence to your interviewers in a professional presentation. You want to make sure your style is friendly, perhaps emulating a teacher you respect who served as a role model for you. Critique your speech and your speaking style, as well. Some interviewers are highly critical of local dialects and what may be perceived as careless articulation. We all can benefit from careful attention to our speech and body language. Develop a regimen of regularly working on this aspect of your presentation. It will enhance your effectiveness at interviews, in your classroom, and throughout your life.

NOTES NOTES NOTES

Your speech quality contributes to your interviewers' perceptions of you as a teacher. The content of your answer will influence them, but the quality of your communication will also play a part. Your voice, its tone, its speed, and its volume can be modulated and controlled to project the image you choose. Now is the time to rehearse using inflections, gestures, and pauses while keeping your voice natural and appropriate for your audience. How do you want them to perceive you? Videotape or audiotape yourself using your responses developed from previous chapters. The following may help you to critique your practiced responses:

- Did I intersperse my thoughts with too many verbal fillers such as "er," "like," "um," and "Do you know what I mean?"
- Did I rush my response? Would it be difficult for people to understand what I said?
- Was my voice pleasant? Do I need to practice keeping it within a conversational range?
- Was my nervousness apparent? Do I have a tendency to get too loud or too quiet?
- Did I vary my delivery to hold the attention of the interviewers?
- Will my interviewers be comfortable with my language style?

Body language can convey thoughts and feelings you might not wish to communicate. Videotaping your practice sessions or observing yourself in front of a mirror can be useful in critiquing your body language. You might want to respond to prepared interview questions in a role-play simulation with a friend who can monitor your behavior. See what gestures you have that you're not aware of. Practice your body language to emphasize and not detract from your message. Consider evaluating yourself using the following questions:

- Do I smile or frown too often?
- Do I keep eye contact with my interviewer?
- Does my nervousness show (e.g., rubbing my hands together, twisting in my seat, or rocking my foot back and forth)?
- Do I fidget with my clothing?

At the interview, your body movements may reveal a great deal about you as a person and how you might act as a teacher. As you walk into the interview, take a deep breath and offer your firm handshake, pleased to have reached this point in your job search. Respond to your interviewer's nonverbal cues. If necessary, clarify or expand your response if you sense something was confusing. Your goal as you practice is to enhance your confidence in your abilities, thereby reducing your anxiety.

CREATING A PROFESSIONAL PRESENCE

When you are called for an interview, you know you have been successful in making a good first impression with your application. You want to add to that positive impression at your interview. Managing your stress, looking the part, planning your nutrition, and planning a timely arrival are critical to preparation for your interview. Your attention to detail will convey an important message.

Managing your stress is an important facet of your communication. We know that interviewing is stressful. It is essential that you have a variety of strategies for managing your feelings. You want to teach your body to relax on cue, helping you cope with the more nerve-racking aspects of the interview process. What follows are a few regimens that some have found useful in presenting a more relaxed, controlled demeanor.

- In a quiet room, attend to your breathing. The goal is to breathe slowly and deeply. Count your breaths. As the time lengthens between each breath you'll begin to relax and feel more at ease.
- You might think of a *mantra,* a few lines of a poem, a prayer, or a song, that you could repeat several times to calm your mood.
- If there is one part of your body that typically gets "out of joint" when you are under pressure, try directing your energy to that point. Alternate tensing and releasing those muscles to relax your body.

You can use one or more of these processes just before, and perhaps even during, your interview. Having practiced the exercises, you'll be able to call on these tools to ease the bothersome aspects of nervousness that can appear when you are under pressure, such as a quivering voice, a soft and inaudible response, excessive gesturing, or a rapid pace.

Looking the part is important as you practice presenting your professional image. Be aware of your personal appearance, your grooming, your demeanor, and your clothing as reflections of your professionalism.

- Is your hair neat?
- Are your fingernails clean?
- Does your walk convey confidence?
- Do your clothes fit comfortably? Are they freshly pressed?
- Are you prepared for a sneeze (tissue) or a dry throat (cough drops)?

You might consider creating two interview outfits that can be used for all of your first interviews. Keep track of what you wear so that you are not later seen in precisely the same outfit. Modifications (e.g., a coordinating tie or shirt) can serve for follow-up contacts. If possible, try to wear clothes you have worn on other occasions, so you know the fit is comfortable and the pockets are handy. The goal here is to select attire that conveys your professional presence and allows you to be yourself as you go through the interview. Two books filled with helpful tips that can guide you are *Dress for Success* and *The Woman's Dress for Success* by John Malloy. Knowing that your clothes are in good order the night before will help you to sleep well.

Planning your nutrition is another detail you need to spend time on. An empty stomach can hinder your thinking processes. For this reason you should eat appropriately before your interview to ensure that your body is energized. Avoid foods that may have lingering aromas or leave telltale messages on your clothes. Don't expect to eat a meal at your interview. You will need to focus all your energy on the conversation, occasionally perhaps sipping on a beverage or snacking on some finger food. If you accept an offer of food or beverage, be prepared to cope with balancing it on your knee or the possibility of spilling. Might it be better to decline? Make that decision based on your comfort level.

Plan a timely arrival. In addition to preparing your wardrobe, you need to get to the interview on time. Your timely arrival will communicate your reliability, your professionalism, and your respect for your interviewers' time. Arriving in advance of your appointment may also allow you to check your appearance and get a sense of the atmosphere in the school building.

The following are important steps you might consider taking:

- Collect relevant information such as maps, routes, and schedules.
- Identify a variety of transportation options; for example, mass transit, personal automobile, or taxi.
- Identify friends or relatives who might offer you a ride.
- Calculate the cost and access the finances needed to borrow a car or use a taxi.
- Estimate the door-to-door transit time, including time to walk or wait for connections to get to the interview site.
- Allow for possible delays and commuter congestion, whether using public transportation or your own car.

NOTES NOTES NOTES

- Make a "dry run" at approximately the same hour and same day of the week as you'll be traveling to your interview.

Be ready to modify your plans to accommodate unanticipated delays. These arrangements should obviously be done well in advance of the interview day.

SUMMING UP

Practicing helps you to anticipate potential obstacles to your smooth presentation. You've identified strategies that allow your mind to respond to many of the events that will occur in rapid succession. Use the inevitable adrenaline rush to sharpen the communication of your ideas, your confidence, and your image. On the day of the interview, you want to arrive early, neatly dressed, well nourished, and ready to convey your strengths. Your systematic preparation will put you in the best position, physically and mentally, to convey your professionalism while you continue to gather information about the position and the school community.

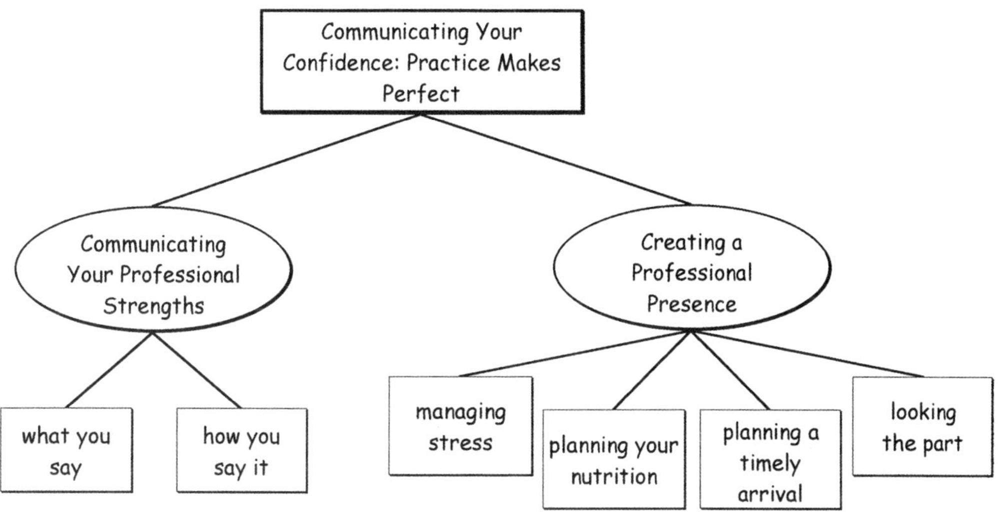

PART E

REFLECTING ON YOUR JOURNEY

Reflecting on your interview is an essential activity to enhance your success at subsequent opportunities. Reflect on Kippi's responses as she proceeds through her interview as preparation for reflecting on your own experiences.

What actually happened at the interview? Which responses do I need to modify? What worked? Chapter 10, Learning From Your Interview, addresses two important issues: strategies for reflecting on your interview and points to consider as you decide if you want to teach at this particular school.

Coming full circle, chapter 11, Continuing the Journey, details useful steps to ensure that your name and application stay at the top of interviewers' lists while you consider your next opportunities.

SCENARIO

KIPPI FRANK

An Initial, School-Based Interview With a Demonstration Lesson

Candidate:	Kippi Frank	
Interviewers:	Mr. Gomez	Principal
	Ms. Gold	Assistant Principal

It is December and the school year at the Tenth Street School is well underway. Ms. Thomas, the star fourth-grade teacher, has informed the administration that she will be leaving because her family is unexpectedly relocating. The administration needs to find a replacement immediately.

WHO IS KIPPI?

Kippi Frank is an undergraduate student minoring in elementary education. She has been a commuter student, maintaining her roots in her community where her family moved when she was in middle school. Kippi is the first person in her family to attend college, and her parents are proud of her decision to become a teacher. Now in her last semester prior to graduation, she is student teaching while actively looking for a teaching position.

There are many schools in her home community, but Kippi is not really familiar with them, having attended elementary school in another section of the city where she lived as a youngster. Her younger brother is a student in the neighborhood middle school, and he helps her understand where the district schools are located.

Kippi has little knowledge of how to find a "good" setting to begin her teaching, but she holds out hope for a school where the students' success is the main priority. Before school started in September, Kippi reviewed the school directory stored at the reserve desk at her college library. After noting the addresses of all the local schools, she sent her résumé to each one.

HOW DID KIPPI GET HER INTERVIEW?

Kippi came home one day to find a message on her answering machine indicating that the Tenth Street School was interested in interviewing her for an expected opening in January. Excited at the prospect of getting a position near her home, Kippi called immediately. Her call was put through to Mr. Gomez, who asked Kippi if she was still looking for a job. On her affirmative response, he suggested that she come for an interview the next morning at 9:00 a.m.

HOW DID KIPPI PREPARE FOR THE INTERVIEW?

Kippi immediately called Tamika, a colleague in student teaching, hoping to share her excitement and brainstorm what to expect, but Tamika was not home. Kippi realized she was becoming increasingly anxious, and then reassured herself that there must have been something about her résumé that impressed them!

Kippi thought about what she would wear, remembering her professor's admonition, "No jeans or jazzy ball gowns." She looked at all the clothes in her closet and pulled out a blue skirt, a print blouse, and a matching blue cardigan. She also selected her dressy heels. Kippi pressed her clothes, knowing that a good first impression is important in the process of getting a teaching post. She checked the condition of her hair and nails, attending to these important details before going to bed. She was ready!

As the school was just down the street, Kippi did not have to be concerned about travel directions or a complex time schedule. She would be in total control of what time she would arrive for her interview.

THE INTERVIEW

At 8:50 a.m. Kippi approached the large doors to the Tenth Street School, where she was met by a security guard. After signing the register, she moved quickly in the direction indicated, making certain that she would not be late for her 9:00 a.m. appointment. She was ushered into the principal's office and told that Mr. Gomez would be back shortly and she should make herself comfortable. Kippi sat down at the chair next to what she assumed was Mr. Gomez's desk.

Mr. Gomez entered with the person who had directed Kippi into the office. Kippi jumped up. Mr. Gomez introduced himself and Ms. Gold, the assistant principal, inviting Kippi to take a seat at the large table. All three of them sat down.

Mr. Gomez: So glad you could come on such short notice, because we've just found out that the husband of one of our highly rated teachers is transferring to a position in Hong Kong, and needless to say, she's going with him. That leaves us with an opening in the fourth grade. Why don't you tell us something about yourself and your background so we can get started. [1]

What inferences might Kippi make from this brief interchange:
1. about the school?
2. about Mr. Gomez?
3. about the teacher to be replaced?

Kippi: I'm just finishing my teacher education program at Mercy University and I'm ready to teach. I student taught in the pre-kindergarten and sixth-grade classes and I found those experiences very exciting. I created a portfolio of some of my accomplishments, but I forgot to bring it. I can go home and get it or I can bring it back later on today, if you'd like. [2]

What has Kippi conveyed about herself and her preparation for this interview?

KEEP IN MIND

[1]Mr. Gomez indicates he realizes that Kippi was accommodating to appear for an interview on short notice. Ordinarily, candidates would be given more time to prepare. He seems to be under some pressure to fill a position unexpectedly and provided much information to Kippi. He describes the current teacher as "highly rated," suggesting that he values good teachers. The opening is in the fourth grade. Mr. Gomez is interested in hearing Kippi talk about herself and her background.

[2]Kippi is proud of her teacher education program and her university. She feels "prepared" to teach, suggesting confidence in her abilities. When discussing her student teaching experience, she mentions pre-kindergarten and sixth grade, despite the fact that Mr. Gomez has specifically indicated an opening in the fourth grade. Although Kippi is telling the truth, she is not offering any basis for Mr. Gomez to assign her to a fourth-grade position.

The fact that she created a portfolio is noteworthy. However, the fact that she did not bring it suggests a lack of organization, perhaps attributable to the limited notice she was given for the interview. Kippi neglects to focus

(continued)

NOTES NOTES NOTES

What information do you think Mr. Gomez is seeking by asking about the portfolio?

Mr. Gomez: That won't be necessary. Why don't you tell us what's in the portfolio? [3]

Kippi: I start with my philosophy of education, what I believe is essential for students to learn and the kinds of settings which are essential for learning. I then have loads of my lesson plans and worksheets which I used with the kids, and lists of books which we used, and a few pictures of the kids in the classroom, the schoolyard, and the lunchroom. At the end, I have some of the cards that the kids sent me on my last day as a student teacher in my first placement. They were so cute. They wished me good luck and all. I really miss them. [4]

How may Kippi's choice of words be perceived by her interviewers?

KEEP IN MIND

her comment, suggesting her portfolio may be more of a general scrapbook than a document supporting her candidacy. Her willingness to return with it indicates pride in her work and enthusiasm to share it. Most important, Kippi has not yet helped them to know her: what her interests are, what her goals are, what her teaching experiences are, or what motivates her to be a teacher, for example.

[3]Mr. Gomez has initially indicated that there was some need for haste in this process of interviewing, so he does not want to wait for her to go home and return. He wants to proceed. He's listening to Kippi's comments and seeking more information about her portfolio. He is asking her to highlight what's important, again allowing her to take the lead. He is looking for evidence of her ability to deal with a fourth-grade classroom, which is his immediate concern.

[4]Kippi has listened carefully to Mr. Gomez's request and has given a general overview of the contents of her portfolio. We have only a vague sense of the types of activities she has highlighted. Describing the students' cards as "cute" sounds superficial. Her comment about missing the students suggests that there is a warm connection between Kippi and her students. Her caring for them is becoming clear, although we cannot be sure of her academic priorities. Mr. Gomez and Ms. Gold may take exception to her consistent use of the word *kids*, believing it suggests a lack of respect.

Mr. Gomez: Your name is such an unusual one. Can you tell us something about how you were named Kippi? [5]

Kippi: Oh, sure! My mother and father had one favorite author, Rudyard Kipling. And so they wanted to use his name when I was born. They clearly couldn't call me Rudyard so they shortened Kipling to Kippi and that's my name! Now I've become an avid Kipling fan; I guess that's a result of my parents' constant reading to me from his stories. And I love to read his works to my students. They never seem to tire of his stories and poems. [6]

Ms. Gold: I notice you have a beautiful diamond ring on your finger. Are you planning to get married soon? [7]

Kippi: Um . . . Yes, my fiancé and I are planning to get married this summer.

NOTES NOTES NOTES

Why is Mr. Gomez asking Kippi about her name? What information do you think she should provide?

How will Kippi's response about Kipling advance her candidacy for the position?

Asking about Kippi's engagement ring is the second personal question. How do you think she should respond?

KEEP IN MIND

[5]Mr. Gomez could be trying to get Kippi to talk more about herself, feeling that she really has not told them much yet. On the other hand, he could believe that by asking about her name he will find out more about Kippi's ethnicity. If the second is true, then this could be perceived as an indication of some potential bias. Kippi will need to consider how she responds to this inquiry so that she accomplishes her objective(s). If her perception matches our hunch that this might suggest an illegal inquiry into her ethnicity as a way to discriminate in a hiring decision, she will need to decide if she will address her ethnicity or if she will respond more neutrally and reveal less about herself personally. Clearly Kippi is likely to have been asked this question at other times in her life, and she can draw on those experiences as she decides what she will say.

[6]Kippi's response has focused on the connection between her name and the position for which she is interviewing. She remarks on how she shares her familiarity with Kipling's work with her students, focusing the conversation on professional issues.

[7]The question could be viewed as one that can help Kippi to be comfortable, relaxed, and sociable, indicating a concern by the administrators for more than the teaching side of an individual. Ms. Gold could be congratulating her or wishing her well with this comment.

(continued)

NOTES NOTES NOTES

Ms. Gold: Do you think that you will want to continue to teach after that? [8]

Kippi: Certainly. I've gone through college just to become a teacher. My fiancé is most supportive of my decision and I know he will help me to be successful. In fact, I frequently tell him about what I'm planning and he comes up with great ideas to make the lessons more exciting. [9]

Mr. Gomez: As we've mentioned, the position we have available is in the fourth grade. What experiences have you had with the fourth-grade curriculum and with fourth graders? [10]

What information do you think Kippi should provide in her response about the fourth-grade curriculum?

KEEP IN MIND

Especially because this comment is coming on the heels of the one about Kippi's name, we're aware that this question could be considered illegal. Kippi will need to respond in some way that will again accomplish her goal. If she thinks she might be interested in the teaching position at this school, despite these two personal inquiries, she needs to be cautious in her response. She wants to avoid offending the interviewers and ending the interview, while being true to herself and her ideals.

[8]Clearly Ms. Gold has not gotten the information she is looking for, causing her to follow up with a specific inquiry about Kippi's long-term plans. Could she be hinting that marriage and teaching might not mix? Kippi has responded respectfully to these questions, revealing little about her personal life. The interviewers, however, seem to want to encroach on her personal life, and she has found a way to make it more difficult for them to do this.

[9]Notice how Kippi responds to the direct question by bringing the interview back to the purpose for all of them being together. She is advancing her access to teaching resources, identifying her fiancé as an additional source of ideas from which to draw as she plans lessons.

[10]Mr. Gomez has returned to the professional issues involved in this interview. He is seeking specific information about Kippi's potential curriculum for a fourth-grade class and her experiences with fourth graders. He is focusing her attention on the fact that this is the only reason they are interviewing her at this time—to consider her as a possible replacement for a fourth-grade teacher. Despite the fact that he specifically mentioned this focus at the start of the interview, Kippi has not offered anything about her knowledge or experience with fourth graders.

Kippi: Not much, really. There was a fourth-grade class next door to my sixth-grade class during student teaching. I talked with the teacher some, and to some of the kids in her class who were real cute. My best friend student taught in a fourth-grade in another school. And then, of course, my work at Mercy included talking about fourth graders—and all of the grades for that matter. [11]

Mr. Gomez: Tell me about the kinds of assessment you would use in your classroom.

Kippi: I wrote a paper on assessment for one of my courses. I got an A on it. It was the best in the class! Assessment is how a teacher knows if kids have achieved specific goals—like the learning standards. Years ago, kids took a test and the teacher corrected it. Only the teacher knew what would be on the test or what was counted as correct. Today there's an emphasis on performance assessment and now kids are more involved with the tasks being more authentic.

I know self-assessment works in the writing process. Kids can be taught to look at their writing to see where they should modify, delete, or add information. They can look for "evidence" of achieving specific goals. Assessment and instruction go hand in hand for me.

In one class where I student taught, the teacher introduced the criteria for evaluation on the very first day she started a new project. She let the kids know what she would be looking for and how she would know if they had learned what she was setting out to teach them. This seemed to work very well in this class. Kids didn't seem to be in the dark about their goals. They seemed to know exactly what was required of them. And then the whole concept of responsibility for their own learning comes into play. I think performance assessment is quite consistent

NOTES NOTES NOTES

List the strengths and limitations of Kippi's answer about her experiences with the fourth-grade curriculum.
Strengths

Limitations

Here's an opportunity to convey your specific knowledge about potential classroom assessment activities. How would you respond?

KEEP IN MIND

[11]While Kippi starts out weakly—with a negative comment—she quickly identifies several sources of her experiences with the fourth grade. The fact that she repeats the use of the word *cute* might suggest that she is focusing on the energy of the students, an important element, but she has not indicated any content or academic focus, which clearly may be a concern for Mr. Gomez. Remembering that her coursework is a source for information and that her best friend student taught in a fourth-grade class, Kippi might access these resources as she prepares for the teaching assignment if she were to get the job.

with the new state standards, particularly for the fourth-grade assessment. [12]

Ms. Gold: Thank you for letting us know your ideas on assessment. Assessment and accountability are very important issues, particularly with the new state tests. You can realize, we've had many applications and we'll need to make a decision fairly quickly. Can you help us by telling us why we should consider you for this position? [13]

This sounds like a culminating question. What should Kippi say to emphasize her qualifications?

Kippi: Well, first off, I live close by, so there won't be any problem with me being here in bad weather. I think I might like the fourth grade, and I am very anxious to get a job so that I can start to teach. I know that student teaching is not really teaching and I am ready for the responsibility of taking on a class by myself. I have a lot of energy and I know I will be a good teacher. [14]

What strengths did Kippi highlight?

KEEP IN MIND

[12]Kippi informed them that she was aware of different models of assessment, particularly stressing her experience with performance assessment. When she placed her conversation within the context of the state standards, she gave evidence of both a need for students to achieve the standards and one part of a multipronged strategy to promote students' performance at the required level of proficiency.

[13]Ms. Gold is trying to help to focus Kippi on the need to impress the interviewers with her credentials: why she should be the "chosen apple" in this highly competitive setting. She is giving Kippi the opportunity to explicitly make a pitch for herself as the one to follow in the footsteps of their departing colleague. Ms. Gold is also offering a sense of the timing of the process so that if Kippi has other "irons in the fire" she would know that this school is planning to work fairly rapidly in coming to closure on a job offer.

An alternative explanation may suggest that Ms. Gold wants to bring the interview to a quick conclusion because she has not pursued any of the statements Kippi made. Perhaps she's unimpressed with Kippi's responses or the philosophy behind her statements.

[14]Kippi's initial remark about her proximity to the school may have sounded flip in this highly formalized setting. On the other hand, she may have been attempting to be more casual. Although location is probably a consideration in a hiring decision, it is unlikely to be the first criterion in selecting a candidate.

(continued)

Mr. Gomez: That's all very helpful. Can you tell us what a typical day might be like in your classroom? [15]

Kippi: Well, I've not really thought very concretely about that yet, not knowing what grade or anything I might get. But in general, I can assure you that I would have a time when I read to the class everyday, maybe right after lunch. I would also have the students create portfolios as the term progresses. I would also ask the parents to help out in class as much as possible. I guess I'll need to get to be more specific, but that's the best I can do right now. [16]

Ms. Gold: That's fine. Is there anything else you think we should know about you before we let you go? [17]

NOTES NOTES NOTES

How would you respond to Mr. Gomez's question about a typical day?

What inferences might Mr. Gomez make about Kippi's professional philosophy?

How might you respond to Ms. Gold's question about providing additional information?

KEEP IN MIND

Kippi's tentativeness about "liking" the fourth grade might be viewed as being less than enthusiastic. She may be conveying her desire to teach while being adaptable in the grade level.

Kippi clearly states her confidence that she will be a good teacher, and that she has a lot of energy, neither of which might have come across so far in the interview. She's implying that she's different when she's with students. Kippi's answer gets stronger as she responds to Ms. Gold's question, realizing that Ms. Gold has provided her with an opportunity to promote her candidacy.

[15]From Kippi's last response, Mr. Gomez seems to have some renewed interest, asking for specific activities she might include in her classroom. He is suggesting that he wants to hear more of her professional ideas.

[16]Kippi consistently starts out negatively. Perhaps this is a defensive tactic or a self-deprecating one. Perhaps she is unprepared and unrehearsed. Her explanation that she's waiting to know the specific grade that she will teach makes sense in general. As we listen to the rest of her response, she identifies her commitment to specific activities regardless of grade level. The activities she identifies clearly focus her energies on enhancing the literacy proficiencies of her students while expanding their knowledge and understanding of themselves as learners. Her desire to include parents in her activities indicates a level of confidence in herself while recognizing the need for accessing important resources. Kippi also indicates that she will need to do specific planning, but at this moment she is not prepared to talk specifically.

[17]Ms. Gold is cuing Kippi that her interview is drawing to a close. She encourages Kippi to provide any additional information before the end.

NOTES NOTES NOTES

What do you think Kippi accomplished in her concluding statement?

Kippi: I'd be real interested in knowing more about the programs you have going here, and what I might be fitting into. I am a very curious person. I am always looking for new ideas, and am very excited about the prospect of being a teacher in your school. I know I will be a good teacher. I hope you will give me a chance to prove myself. [18]

What inference may Kippi draw from the mention of a demonstration lesson?

Mr. Gomez: You've given us a lot of information and we really appreciate your coming here on such short notice. We sometimes require a quick demonstration lesson of our new hires. Would you be willing to do that for us? [19]

How would you respond to the opportunity to conduct a demonstration lesson?

Kippi: Sure! [20]

Mr. Gomez: Well, you'll be hearing from us. Thanks so much for coming in.

KEEP IN MIND

[18]Kippi has given evidence of being an interested candidate, wanting to know more about the school. Her characterization of herself as "always looking for new ideas" suggests that she is open to considering alternatives and willing to try new projects. She says that she is excited about the prospect of being a teacher in the school, explicitly stating her feelings and leaving no uncertainty about her desire to be seriously considered as a candidate.

Kippi realizes that this is her opportunity to make a last and lasting impression. She wants to make sure that her interviewers know that she wants this position by explicitly telling them about herself, in contrast to her earlier, understated comments. Mr. Gomez and Ms. Gold might also infer (correctly!) that this is Kippi's first interview and that she is very nervous.

[19]Although ignoring Kippi's request for more information about the school, Mr. Gomez seems sincere in his comments, acknowledging that Kippi has offered useful information. He is particularly appreciative of her availability on short notice. His comment about the possibility of a demonstration lesson suggests that he may consider her as a potential teacher, or more precisely, that she has not been eliminated from the selection or screening process. Mr. Gomez is "testing the waters" with Kippi to see whether, at this point, she's still interested.

[20]Kippi's immediate, unequivocal response suggests that she is both comfortable with Mr. Gomez and Ms. Gold and really interested in working in their school.

When Kippi got home, she called Tamika again, hoping to get some insights about what to expect in a fourth-grade class, where Tamika was currently student teaching. She would ask Tamika for ideas for a demonstration lesson. Tamika was excited for Kippi and offered some possibilities.

NOTES NOTES NOTES

THE DEMONSTRATION LESSON

The next morning Ms. Gold called Kippi and invited her to come for a 20-minute demonstration lesson at 2:15 p.m. that afternoon with the fourth-grade class. Kippi was excited about the opportunity. She knew one thing for sure: She would bring her portfolio this time!

Kippi was surprised at the limited preparation time. Fortunately, she had given some thought to what she and Tamika had discussed if she were called back. She listed some materials and books she would use, but she had not collected these yet. She needed to work quickly. As she thought more specifically about the lesson, she realized that she didn't know how many students would be there, how the classroom was organized, what resources were available, what they were working on currently, or really anything about the students except that they were assigned to a fourth-grade class.

Luckily, Kippi found a book of short stories on her shelf and decided that she would read one of these to the class and then ask them to compare the story with one of their own experiences. She also listed some vocabulary words that might cause difficulty. She looked at the list of five vocabulary words she had identified and realized that she could pare down the list and emphasize one that might be problematic for the students' understanding of the plot.

She planned to review this essential word before reading. Following the reading she would ask them to write their own stories if there was time. Maybe they could write stories in small groups. Knowing that she only had a total of 20 minutes to work with the students, Kippi had selected the shortest story. She practiced reading slowly and dramatically, gaining confidence as she read, observing her presentation in her mirror. With her storybook, lesson plan, and portfolio in hand, she arrived at the school at 2:00 p.m., allowing a little time to get settled before teaching the class. [21]

What does Kippi's plan reveal about her understanding of teaching, children's concept development, and literacy development?

[21]Kippi's planning included several activities during this 20-minute minilesson. Choosing a story that she thought would be of interest to the students, she created ways for them to deal with its content conceptually. She practiced reading

(continued)

Plan of Action

Discuss meaning of vocabulary word	2 minutes
I will read the story	6 minutes
We will talk about the story	3 minutes
Start to write their own stories	6 minutes
Sharing stories	3 minutes

Kippi waited for Mr. Gomez, reading the story slowly to herself, trying to calm her nerves.

Ms. Gold: Oh, there you are! I was hoping you'd come to my office so that we could talk a little about the students in the class but I guess there's no time for that now. Let's go on to Ms. Thomas's room, just down the hall here. Ms. Thomas is the teacher we told you about. She's really wonderful with the students and they do so well with her. Well, I guess we've been lucky working with her these past 6 years. Now we have an opening—and maybe you'll be the next person we talk about just as we talk about Ms. Thomas.

At 2:15 p.m. Mr. Gomez entered Ms. Thomas's room along with Ms. Gold and Kippi.

Ms. Thomas: We have a visitor today who's going to do something special with you. Please give her your best attention.

Kippi: Hi. My name is Kippi and I'm so happy to be here with you today for this brief visit. I've brought along a story that I really like, and I hope you will too. [22]

KEEP IN MIND

the story aloud so that her presentation is conducive to students' understanding. She has selected one word that she thinks might be essential in their understanding of the story and created a context to focus their attention.

Her dramatic oral reading of the story will both energize the students and facilitate their understanding. Her brief time for discussion limits the opportunity for individual response, allowing Kippi to more carefully control the activities of the students. Kippi decided that Mr. Gomez and Ms. Gold wanted to see her presentation style in the classroom, not her real teaching ability.

She knew it would be impossible to actually teach anything of great significance in 20 minutes, particularly with students she had never met before. Teaching at the end of the day and lacking information about the students are clear handicaps, but Kippi does not balk at these circumstances. She is showing that she can "go with the flow."

[22]Kippi is presenting a very positive, energetic stance. Her desire to share with the students seems to be consistent with the persona she talked about in her interview with Mr. Gomez and Ms. Gold. *(continued)*

First, I'd like to review one vocabulary word with you, just to make sure we will all understand the story. (Writing the word on the board . . .) Camouflage . . . Who knows the word camouflage? (Seeing many hands raised, she nods to one student)

NOTES NOTES NOTES

Student 1: It's a way to hide.

Student 2: Sometimes animals camouflage themselves when they are afraid of getting killed.

Kippi: Okay. It seems like you know this word. Knowing that camouflage is an important concept in this story, who has some ideas about what the story might be about?

Kippi proceeded to call on several students and then read the story. At the end of her reading, she asked what they thought of the story. After several answers like "It was good," and "It was okay," Kippi asked them to write their own story about camouflage. The students took out paper as Kippi walked around the room. There were several student inquiries, such as, "Do we do it by ourselves?" and "Can we do it as a class?"

Kippi: Okay. You can work in pairs with the person next to you. [23]

Ms. Thomas (to Kippi): There's no more time left. The children need to get ready for dismissal.

Kippi: I'm sorry, boys and girls, but the time is up. I hope you will have time to work on your stories some more. I'd love to read them. Perhaps Ms. Thomas will send them to me. Thanks so much. (Kippi took her book in hand and walked out of the room.)

Ms. Gold: (following Kippi out of the room) Thank you for your lesson. We'll be in touch.

KEEP IN MIND

In this setting where Ms. Thomas, Mr. Gomez, and Ms. Gold are the names she's heard, Kippi might want to introduce herself more formally, as Ms. Frank. Not all schools are comfortable with students calling teachers by their first names.

[23]Kippi listens and responds to student inquiries. The students' questions may suggest that Kippi has not provided adequate directions about the goals of the activity and their options. They also suggest that the students are seeking to be responsive to her requests, perhaps evidencing reciprocal respect.

SUMMING UP

Clearly Kippi's résumé must have impressed Mr. Gomez and Ms. Gold in some way. However, their reason for selecting her application is not explicitly stated or inquired about. Something moved her application to the top of the pile. Perhaps it was just that she was conveniently located to the school. There were many opportunities to potentially impress them with her professional qualifications:

- Enthusiastic about becoming a teacher, evidencing high energy.
- Values students and taps their concerns and knowledge.
- Conveys a positive, optimistic perspective about her abilities.
- Articulates a clear philosophy and related activities she would include in her classroom.
- Is resourceful in seeking ideas.

Kippi needs to consider how she will follow up on this experience.

Overall, she believes she exhibited her professional qualifications that will earn her a place in the Tenth Street School:

P – Portfolio, plans
L – Learning, literature
A – Assessment
C – Curiosity
E – Energy

CHAPTER 10 LEARNING FROM YOUR INTERVIEW

AT A GLANCE

In this chapter we help you to systematically learn from your interviews by recording details of all that occurred and then reflecting on and interpreting the events. This combination of activities is essential in anticipation of being asked back, contemplating the goodness of fit between you and the school, and preparing for additional opportunities.

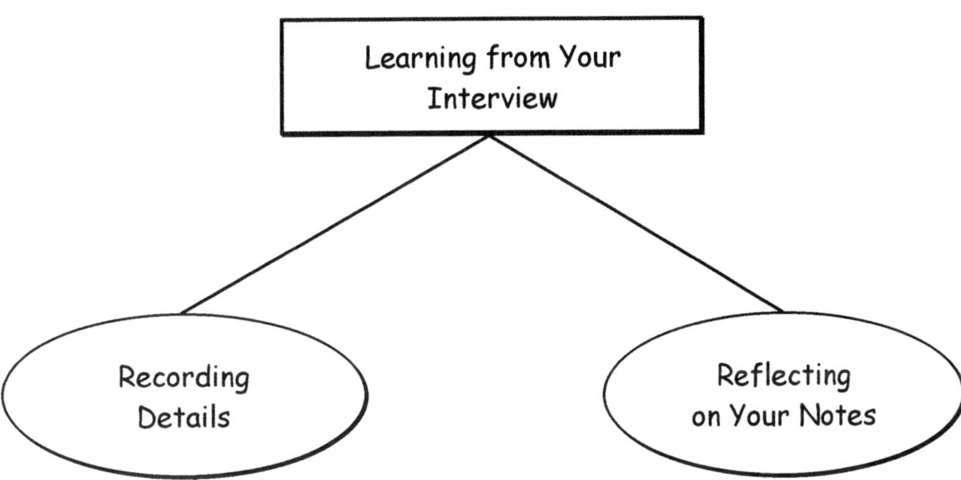

NOTES NOTES NOTES

Although you have succeeded at getting an interview, you cannot afford to relax. You will need to become self-critical about this event, which is not an easy task. To help you learn from your interview, we start with sample reflections. Then we offer you a systematic process for recalling and recording the details.

To reflect on this process, you want to recall what actually happened, and you want to be as precise as possible. Your detailed record will guide you in finding ways to enhance your chances of success at this and subsequent interviews.

RECORDING DETAILS

We start with sample reflections from Steve, Jennifer, Felicia, Marcy, and Kippi. In these sample reflections our candidates considered their strengths, their areas to improve, and their chances of being hired.

STEVE

I was good! I really felt at home there! I answered the questions well—particularly about why I wanted to teach there! It was really good that I was able to include the information about my Saturday visit and conversations, because I think Mr. Erickson perceives me as being resourceful, with clear ideas, but also open to new ideas.

I think the fact that he asked me to substitute teach is a good sign. But I can't believe that I actually responded that I hadn't thought much about classroom organization, when I know that's not really true. I guess I was taken off guard, and now I know I have serious homework to do—both to communicate the importance of organization when I am substituting, as well as to be able to articulate my ideas clearly and succinctly at another interview.

Because I know I will be called for some substitute teaching, I need to develop some broad-based lessons for different grade levels and I need to explore some good children's literature to use when presenting these lessons. I'm sure Mr. Erickson will look at my organization as I am teaching. At future interviews I will need to provide clearer answers to questions about my philosophy and how I might organize my classroom, what it might look like and how it might function. I guess Mr. Erickson expects to have at least one opening or Ms. Taffel would not have recommended I contact him. But if I restrict myself to considering only one school or one grade, I'll be limiting my opportunities. I'll need to prepare carefully for the substitute teaching experience. I know I'll ask for help from my cooperating teacher and my professors.

JENNIFER

I responded well to the literacy question. I think they liked my ideas about the listening center and the writing center and how I'll use them in my classroom. I really was in control at the interview, mentioning my amateur photography experience and how I'll bring it into the classroom. I was even prepared for the "worst day" question and showed how I learned from that experience. I probably should outline a "best day" scenario in case someone asks me about that. I can go back to some of my old lesson plans to help me remember.

FELICIA

I am so happy I was able to use my portfolio to demonstrate my teaching and learning experiences. I am pleased with most of the responses but I regret that I was not more thorough with the classroom organization question. I could have devoted more time to my ideas about a system of classroom management. I might have included a discussion of the physical setting of my ideal classroom and my views about including students in setting up class rules. I could have discussed my ideas about rewards and consequences, just as I would present the notion to students at the beginning of the year.

I need to rewrite my response to a classroom organization question to include these important points. I need to rehearse these for my next interview so that I include these. Perhaps I need to revisit my mnemonic so that it is more useful for me. I am proud of my performance during the role play, particularly that I was able to recollect an incident that happened when I had taken over the class at the end of last term. I hope they call me again.

MARCY

I may get offered this position! I was enthusiastic. I was confident. I wanted to get to know my interviewers and for them to get to know me. I let them know I'm "into" children: I know what interests them. I'm resourceful. I go after whatever my students need. I'm organized and I let them know I have confidence to manage a classroom full of youngsters.

MARCY *(continued)*

But I know I did not respond to the two or three principals who are looking for a more controlled and controlling philosophy of teaching and learning. I will make a chart for myself of "trigger" cue words and phrases I might use, such as when asked about classroom management. I have a lot of ideas about classroom organization and I've even tried them in student teaching. But I failed to mention these because I had not clearly formulated a response connecting the organization of instruction to students' learning. These principals might prefer someone who is more discipline-oriented. They may want someone more mature and seasoned. Now, the question is: Do I really want to teach in a district where they don't share my values about teaching and learning?

Next time I'll need to analyze each question more fully and respond with more information. I need to consider clearly outlining my strategies when they ask about struggling learners. I want to make sure an interview committee will have an accurate picture of who I am and how I perceive myself as a teacher. Overall I am pleased with the way I answered most of the questions. I was good!

KIPPI

I guess they're seriously considering me since they wanted me to do a demonstration lesson—but the lesson was at 2:15 in the afternoon, when most classes are getting ready to clean up and pull together all of their activities for the day—not a great time for me to intrude on their time. Did they really expect me to do anything in 15 minutes??? Was this a mere formality? Was I really being seriously considered? It's so hard to understand what is happening here. I think I showed them that I had some good ideas for sharing literature with children and getting them to think about what they've heard. I was really good at listening to the students—and encouraging them to work together, especially because that made the project more likely to get done in such a short time.

I'll need to be more careful in my planning next time. Maybe I need to look at the other schools I applied to and find materials that may be appropriate for their students. I could bring the materials to the interview, and given the opportunity for a demonstration lesson, I could actually use them with the children. This might be a good way to impress another school. In the interim, I wonder if I can expect to get any feedback from Ms. Gold about the lesson. I also need to be more organized on the day of the interview, so that I don't forget my portfolio if I'm planning to bring it. And I need to highlight some key parts of the portfolio: Most people won't take the time to read through the whole document.

These samples focus on different elements of the experience. Some are highly organized, whereas others seem almost "stream of consciousness" in form. The range of formats suggests the diverse styles represented among the applicants.

NOTES NOTES NOTES

Just as Steve, Jennifer, Felicia, Marcy, and Kippi recorded their thoughts after their interviews, you, too, will benefit from each of your interviews by carefully reflecting on them. To expedite that process, we will help you create a review process that accommodates your personal style. We suggest some systematic ways to recall the details of your experience and to organize your reflections.

You might use a generic outline to document your activities, or you might record your immediate recollections on tape as you leave, noting the names of the people you met and their positions. The goal is to recall as many details as possible as soon as possible. You may free write or you may find that an outline prompts your memory (see Fig. 10.1).

My Interview Notes

Date________________ **School______________________________**

PEOPLE I MET

TITLE **RESPONSIBILITY**

Administrators:

Teachers and Specialists:

Parents and Others:

ACTIVITIES

Introductions:

Questions posed and my responses (turn over for more space):

Writing sample - topic - issues:

Departure comments:

INFORMATION TO REMEMBER Re: THE POSITION & THE SCHOOL

For Subsequent Interviews At this School **For Interviews At Other Schools**

MY REACTIONS TO THE PEOPLE, DISCUSSION, AND EVENTS

FIG. 10.1. Sample form for my interview notes.

At first, just focus on recording the interactions. Write! Write! Write! Your notes are likely to be disorganized but will help you to avoid "losing" anything. Subsequently you can identify the accurate sequence of events and create an informal outline of your questions and answers. Although you may not remember everything, you will at least have some materials on which to reflect.

You will probably find that as you review your account, more details will emerge, which you can add to your original notes. If you can construct a virtual transcript of these interactions, you will be in an exceptional position to consider what exactly happened. You may recall, for example, that someone started writing furiously, or another person excused himself, never to return. Documenting the context in which these events occurred may prove important.

These jottings will help as you analyze the interview. Admittedly it is impossible to be objective about one's presentation, but with time, and the distance provided by time and the written word, you are creating a setting in which to effectively critique your interview. You should also note additional information you have now acquired about this particular school in your application file so that all your records relating to this position are together and current. Using the Keep in Mind reflections in the interview scenarios as models, we will help you to reflect on your notes.

REFLECTING ON YOUR NOTES

With your written reconstruction of the interview, you are now ready to interpret your experience using three major questions:

- Will I be called back for a subsequent interview . . . a demonstration lesson . . . a writing sample . . . or will I be eliminated from the pool of potential candidates?
- What have I learned from this interview to improve my performance next time?
- Is this school for me?

We address each of these in turn.

Will I be called back for a subsequent interview . . . a demonstration lesson . . . a writing sample . . . or will I be eliminated from the pool of potential candidates?

The amount of time your interviewers dedicated to your interview may be used as a criterion in assessing the immediate impact you have made. Frequently, the longer the interview, the more likely you are considered a serious candidate. (We assume this was not a courtesy interview, giving you practice but no real expectation of employment; nor was it a sham interview with the successful candidate already determined.) Some settings, however, traditionally dedicate little time to interviews regardless of the impression the candidate is making. In such places, a brief interview is not necessarily indicative of a rejection.

As you said "Goodbye" and "Thank you," and firmly shook hands with your interviewers, you may recall some comments: "It was so nice to meet you." "I look forward to seeing you again soon." "You'll be hearing from us soon!" "Good luck!" Although these comments may seem trivial, they actually may offer a clue as to whether you made a favorable impression on each of your interviewers. The "Good luck!" comment might suggest the person does not envision you as a colleague and is wishing you luck elsewhere. The person who emphasized looking forward to seeing you soon, on the other hand, seems eager to continue the conversation, perhaps as colleagues.

If, on your departure, there is an arrangement for an interview with the superintendent or an appointment for a demonstration lesson, clearly your candidacy is still viable from the interviewers' stance. Typically, however, there is no such commitment at the end of the interview. This is particularly true when it is a "committee" decision in contrast to a single person's decision. There may be other, less explicit clues that may give you a sense of the future.

If you have made a positive impression on some people, but not necessarily the most influential person, you may find that you are not invited to return. Alternatively, if the decision maker is pleased with your presentation, you may have a strong advocate who prevails in your eventual appointment. Keep in mind that there are many people who participate in the process of making a decision.

As you evaluate your experience, consider some of the characteristics of teaching candidates who succeeded in getting the job, as noted in Fig. 10.2. Use this checklist to note the characteristics you communicated as you met with your interviewers. In addition, you might want to note areas where you did not adequately convey these important qualities.

You might also want to return to the original job announcement and evaluate the match between your experiences and those being specifically sought by the district. Comparing these criteria with the added information obtained at the interview may provide important insights for you in assessing the likelihood that there will be a positive follow-up to your interview. Although the ultimate response is difficult to predict, the greater the

Candidate's Name ______________ Interview Date ____________

Teaching Qualities

Qualities	Evidence
confidence	
knowledgeable about: teaching and learning - how people learn - organizing for learning learners' interests learners' needs - standards -content - personal beliefs, values - the educational system - current happenings	
collegial, professional	
articulate	
resourceful, multi-faceted	
inquisitive	
respectful, patient	
energetic	
optimistic	
organized	

Additional Comments:

FIG. 10.2. Checklist of teaching qualities.

match between your credentials and the district's needs, the greater the likelihood that you will be the successful applicant.

What have I learned from this interview to improve my performance next time?

Most often there will be no explanation of why your interview was either successful or unsuccessful. This phenomenon is frustrating, but a savvy applicant critically reviews every step to identify some potentially critical incidents. Your reconstructed interview puts you in a prime position to evaluate how well you presented yourself. You have listed the questions and your responses. Now, use the mnemonic you created to remind you of the major issues you wanted to convey and to evaluate your success in communicating them. Refer to your notes to address all the issues you intended.

Use this opportunity to identify times when you may have spoken in haste, given confusing or incomplete answers, or otherwise poorly presented yourself. As you reflect on the quality of your interactions with the people you met, consider both what you did and what you didn't do or say:

- What did I do well?
- What did I do poorly?
- In what ways did I convince them that I was a good candidate?
- How well did I communicate my ability to address the school's concerns?
- What was I doing or saying at times when the interviewers seemed eager to listen to me?
- What was I doing or saying at times when the interviewers seemed uninterested?
- Which of my statements, documents, or actions contributed to my getting this interview? What's my basis for making this assumption?
- Did people seem interested in finding out about me as a person?
- What did I discover about this school?
- Did the group seem to have similar goals or were there diverse perspectives represented among the participants?
- Did I communicate my major concerns?
- What do they perceive as my main weaknesses?

As you reflect on your interview, identify areas you want to improve on at subsequent interviews. You may realize that you can highlight your experiences in new ways. You may also applaud your ability to respond coherently to unexpected questions. Recognizing that the application process is a cyclical one, revise your application documents using the insights you have developed in this analysis. This will prepare you for your next interview!

Is this school for me?

Your ruminations, along with the other information you have collected about the district, will guide your decision to continue pursuing the post or to eliminate it from further consideration. Although it is impossible to know precisely what each school is looking for (sometimes they don't even know themselves), you are now in a better position to know about the match between your qualifications and the concerns of the school. You want to work where they want you to join their staff. Are you now able to visualize yourself working at the school? You need to decide whether to continue to pursue this position or focus your energies on finding a different opportunity. Some issues to consider include these:

- Do I believe that this would be a good school for me? Why? Why not? Friendly colleagues? Supportive conditions (men-

NOTES NOTES NOTES

toring, small classes, adequate salary, sufficient resources)? Program compatibility? Geographic convenience? Grade level? Size of school?

- Do I have anything to lose by continuing to pursue this position?

You may believe that teaching in this school, although not ideal, offers a chance to make a contribution to students' lives. With such a stance, you may leave your options open, deferring an ultimate decision until a later time.

If your systematic reflections suggest this is not likely to be a good match for you, then you have two choices:

- After sending your thank-you letter, take a wait-and-see attitude, thinking that whenever they get back to you is time enough for you to decide if you want to take this further.
- Explicitly request in a formal letter that your application be withdrawn from further consideration.

SUMMING UP

When the interview ends, you have a serious task ahead of you. You will systematically reflect on your experience and then interpret these reflections to plan your next steps. If you think this is the perfect place for you, you need to ensure that you unambiguously convey your belief to the decision makers.

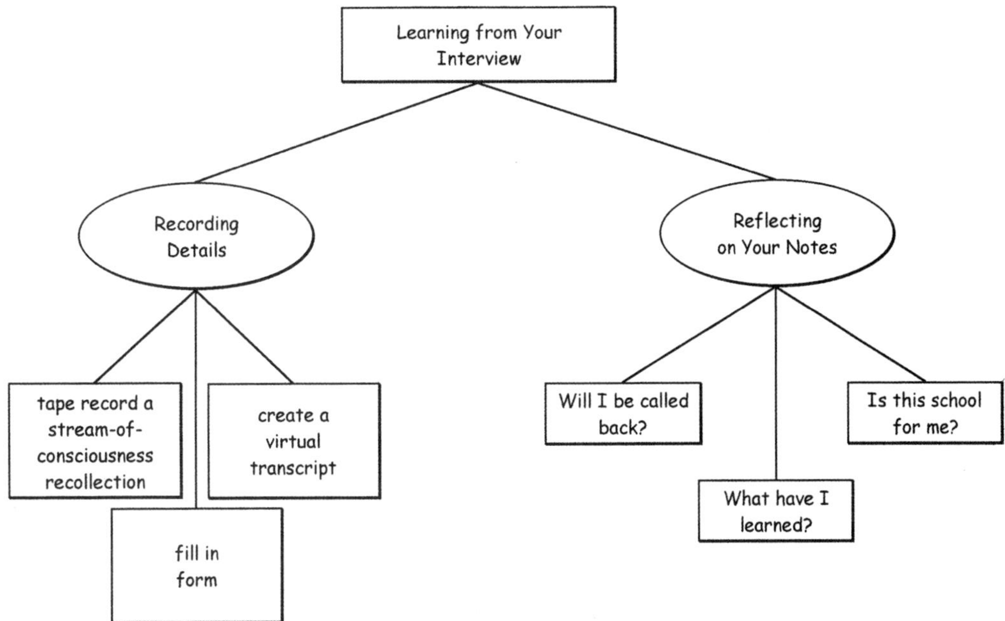

CHAPTER 11 CONTINUING THE JOURNEY

AT A GLANCE

After the interview there are important tasks for you to address. You will follow up and also begin with new applications. We will identify specific activities:

- Alerting references.
- Communicating with the school.
- Reviewing your documents.
- Revisiting your application file.

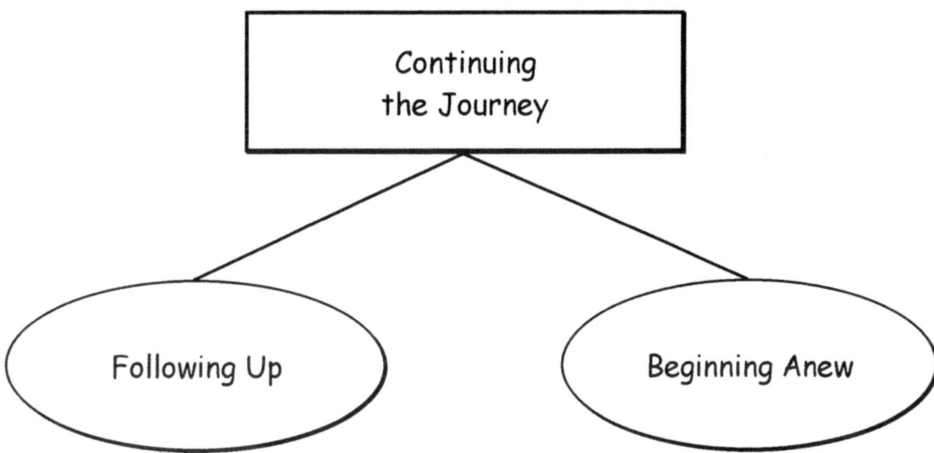

NOTES NOTES NOTES

Good for you: You've completed your interview and learned from it. Remember that the pattern of the search is cyclical. There are still some steps as you follow up with that school and consider your next application. We first address the issue of how to follow up with the school before looking at possibilities in other settings.

FOLLOWING UP

There are two specific tasks for you to attend to immediately following your interview. You will want to alert your references so that they might be available if there is a phone call from the school. You will want to communicate with the school to let them know of your continuing interest in working with them.

Alerting references after your interview is a priority. Call the people you cited as references to let them know they might be hearing from the school. Because you already asked for permission to use their names, your call will not be a shock or require a lengthy conversation. It is simply a reminder that you are still looking for a teaching position and a notice of your recent interview. You want to emphasize the name of the school that may be calling them. To help focus your references' attention when they are being asked about you, mention some experiences that seemed to interest your interviewers and reflect the priorities of the school.

Contact influential individuals who may be in a position to contribute to the decision-making process; possibilities include the parent of a friend who serves on the school board, some colleagues who student taught in that school, or a friend who teaches there now. You may ask their advice on how to promote your application. Keep adding to the pool of people who may be informally contacted for their assessment of you. They may strengthen your chances of landing the job.

Communicating with the school is your next priority. Being mindful that there are likely to be numerous applicants competing for the same position, you need to promote your own success. You want to keep the district interested in your qualifications by following up in different ways: sending a one-page letter, registering for substitute teaching, and regularly reminding them of your continuing interest in working with them. Remember that your interviewers are busy people with limited time to dedicate to this activity. Be brief and direct in your communications.

Send follow-up letters as soon as possible. Your objectives are four-fold:

- To express appreciation for the interview.

- To convey your continuing interest in working at the school.
- To promote the value of your unique characteristics to meet the school's priorities.
- To clarify any potentially murky issues that you now can communicate more effectively and accurately.

If there were multiple interviewers, you will have to decide to whom to send the follow-up letter. How do you decide? Perhaps you'll send the letter to the chair of the search committee; perhaps you'll send it to the person who arranged for the interview or to the person who appeared to be in charge of asking the questions. Be mindful to send your letter promptly.

Your follow-up letter may include the date and time of your interview and one or two sentences about something that was discussed, such as the reading program, to remind the reader who you are. Alternatively, you could mention one of their school projects that would benefit from your strengths. Take the opportunity to clarify or expand on a statement you made at your interview that your reflection leads you to believe was inadequate. These actions restate your desire to work in this school and keep your name current.

Arrange to serve as a substitute teacher by mentioning your desire to be considered in your follow-up letter. Substitute teaching is one guaranteed way to let the administration see some of your abilities with a class. If an interviewer suggests that you register for the substitute list, make arrangements immediately—before departing the building, if possible. If the topic does not come up at your interview, inquire about placing your name on the list.

You might consider some ramifications of subbing in light of any practices you have discovered in researching the school. In areas where substitute teachers are in great demand, your willingness to substitute could weaken your candidacy for a permanent position. In one school you may be valued only as a substitute teacher. On the other hand, subbing may be the typical avenue to a permanent position. Gather information about the school's practice when making your decision regarding substitute teaching.

Convey continuing interest by inquiring about the status of the search or if any additional openings have developed. Allow time to accommodate the screening process but be persistent in your calls. Frequently the secretary or assistant principal is a key resource in this regard. Ask for permission to call at a time when information may be available. Once you get permission, be sure to make the call. Make it understood that you are just seeking information. Keep the call brief so you are not perceived as a nuisance. Because the networks within education can be fairly extensive, you might also inquire about your contacts' knowledge of positions in other schools.

BEGINNING ANEW

Because there are no guarantees about the outcome of any deliberations, particularly the outcome of an interview, it is essential that you make sure you still have some "irons in the fire," some real possibilities, and some real job offers. We recently spoke with a candidate who went through seven interviews, all seemingly successful, yet only the seventh resulted in a job offer. Because this woman was tenacious in her job search, she was proficient at finding opportunities. It's time to review your documents and revisit your application file.

Reviewing your documents will start the cycle once more. After each interview, record new information in your application file. Note the names of the people you interviewed with, their roles, and the specific programs and issues that became evident at your interview. You spent considerable time before the interview getting your documents in order, and you need to spend some time after your interview reviewing them in light of the questions that were asked. Your review will address three documents: your cover letter, résumé, and portfolio.

It is safe to say that your cover letter was acceptable because you were successful at getting the interview. A good reason for revisiting is to confirm that the cover letter introduces you in the best possible light. With your interview experience and future interviews in mind, think about questions and comments that were posed. Were you surprised at statements such as "What did you actually do in your student teaching?" or "I didn't realize you used cooperative learning." Comments like these prompt you to clarify those items that caused some doubt.

Your résumé should be explicit. If you can identify what caused your résumé to rise to the top of the pile, by all means go back and highlight those items. Adjust the presentation of both your cover letter and your résumé to reflect your interview experience.

Review your portfolio to make sure each topic is easy to find. Verify that the issues raised by the interviewers are clearly addressed. If there is a glaring omission, revise your portfolio in light of your review. After you have completed the revisions of your primary documents (cover letter, résumé, portfolio) have a colleague, reliable friend, or relative review them for typographical errors and omissions. (See chap. 4, Assembling Your Application Documents, for further guidance.)

As you continue revisiting your application file you should reconsider job postings you may have put aside and districts you have yet to contact. Perhaps now is the time to initiate a second cycle by submitting additional applications, always keeping at least three to five sites active.

Note the actions needed to keep your files current:

- Follow-up phone calls.
- Requests to send your credential file to the district.
- Close old applications.
- Open new ones.

You want to have your résumé in the hands of all the districts where you would like to teach. Just as you did in your first round, consider hand-delivering your résumé. Recognize the possibility of an immediate interview or the addition of your name to the substitute list as opportunities to make a professional statement or impression. It is possible that the secretary who accepts your résumé will have an influential role in the process. Remember to act like the teacher you want to be.

SUMMING UP

You know that the job search is a cyclical one. Keep the cycle alive. Follow up immediately after your interview and continue to gather and review advertisements, job postings, and newspaper listings. Don't stop looking for a position until you have solid evidence of being hired—a letter of intent or a contract—in hand. Be persistent and you will find the right match.

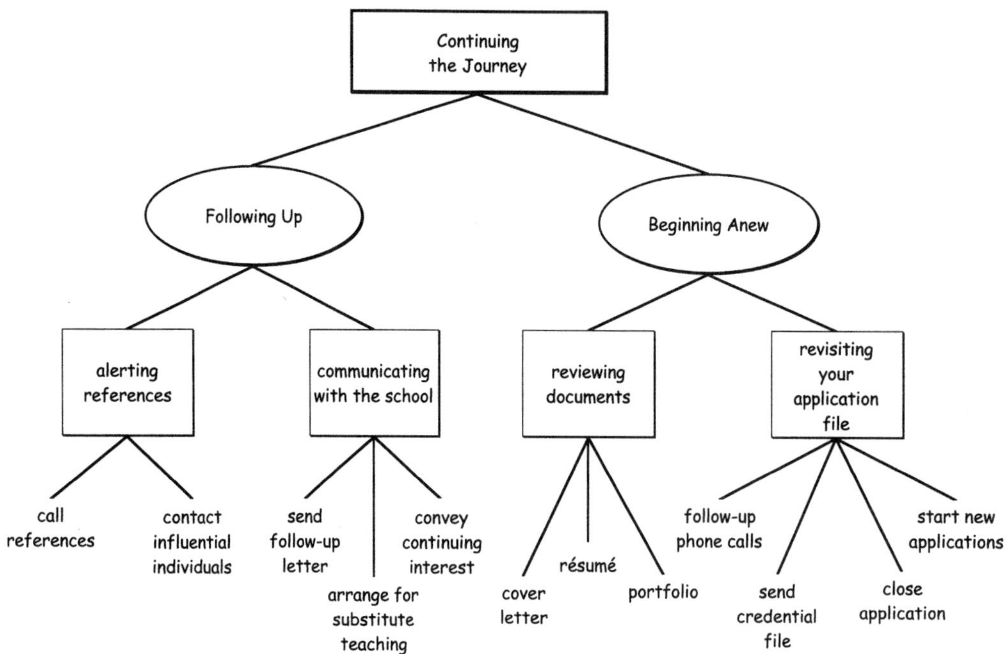

EPILOGUE

Success!

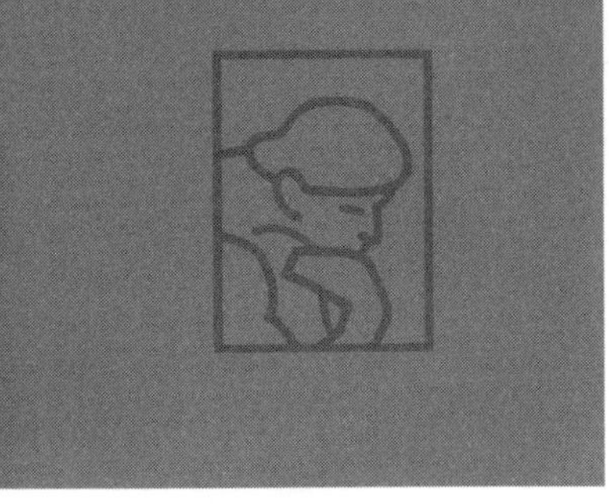

SUGGESTED READINGS

Belenky, M., Blythe, C., Goldberger, N., & Tarule, J. (1986). *Women's ways of knowing: The development of self, voice, and mind.* New York: Basic Books.

This now-classic research study explores women's thinking, documenting the numerous contextual factors that come into play as women negotiate living in a complex, male-dominated society. The findings highlight the importance for organizing classrooms in ways that respond to the numerous styles of interaction that (male and female) students use as they become increasingly responsible for creating their lives.

Brause, R. S. (1992). *Enduring schools: Problems and possibilities.* London: RoutledgeFalmer.

The reader develops an understanding of the impact of school rituals from students' and teachers' perspectives. Encouraging the rethinking of some of these practices, Brause offers windows on authentic classroom organizations and experiences that enhance students' learning.

Clark, C. M. (1995). *Thoughtful teaching.* New York: Teachers College Press.

Clark takes us on a journey on which we envision how to create our schools and classrooms to have the time to listen to our students, understand their needs and interests, and create opportunities to engage our students' minds and spirits as they learn. In the process, he advocates that teachers adopt a teacher–researcher stance for deeper understanding of this complex activity of teaching.

Dewey, J. (1938). *Experience and education.* New York: Macmillan.

Drawing on students' experiences as the basis for communal learning in a classroom setting, Dewey advocates project-based activities that actively engage students while they are simultaneously acquiring increasing proficiency in important skills in a democratic setting. This classic is a must-read.

Duckworth, E. (1987). *"The having of wonderful ideas" and other essays on teaching and learning.* New York: Teachers College Press.

This important book brings together Piaget and the school curriculum. Duckworth's enlightening and entertaining book conveys her belief that intellectual development is a matter of having wonderful ideas and feeling confident to try them out. She provides suggestions for schools having a major impact on the continuing development of ideas (for students and teachers) – an essential ingredient for learning.

Himley, M., & Carini, P. F. (2000). *From another angle: Children's strengths and school standards.* New York: Teachers College Press.

Assessing students' work is a constant concern for teachers. Himley and Carini offer important perspectives on this issue, guiding the readers to understand the characteristics of each student's thinking and offering insights into how to promote continued learning based on this information.

Kohn, A. (1999). *The schools our children deserve: Moving beyond traditional classrooms and "tougher standards."* Boston: Houghton Mifflin.

Kohn is a prominent advocate of constructivist learning and supports his position by presenting both related research and examples from current classrooms. He shows how active learning, based on Dewey and Piaget, can be accomplished. This book offers an important counter position to the educational standards movement.

Kozol, J. (2000). *Ordinary resurrections: Children in the years of hope.* New York: Crown.

We come to understand the children in our urban classrooms from their own words in this inspiring, powerful book. Their optimism propels teachers to create classroom settings that respond to these students' idealism.

Ohanian, S. (1995). *Ask Ms. Class.* Portland, ME: Stenhouse.

Offering thoughtful, realistic responses to important questions about organizing your classroom and all the other issues you wish you knew the answer to, Ohanian will quickly become a savior to a new teacher.

Peters, W. (1987). *A class divided.* New Haven, CT: Yale University Press.

This book describes a classroom exercise designed by Jane Elliott, a third grade Iowa teacher, that helped her students understand the effects of discrimination. The extent of the impact of personalized discrimination was shown in the reactions of the children and their conversations during a reunion fourteen years later.

Rose, M. (1989). *Lives on the boundary*. New York: Penguin.

Rose, M. (1995). *Possible lives: The promise of public education in America*. Boston: Houghton Mifflin.

After describing the impact of individual teachers on his own transformation from disinterested student to scholar in *Lives on the Boundary*, Rose traveled throughout the United States and examined the efforts of caring teachers in their classrooms. He documents the culture of successful classrooms and characteristics of teachers who sustain and empower students.

Sizer, T. R. (1996). *Horace's hope: What works for the American high school*. Boston: Houghton Mifflin.

Sizer addresses the successes and the continuing problems that plague school reform agendas. He reflects on many initiatives, including interdisciplinary learning and inquiry learning in newly configured, extended blocks of time. Ultimately, he is optimistic that school reform, at a critical crossroad, is achievable and worthy of teachers' total efforts.

Spring, J. (2000). *The universal right to education: Justification, definition, and guidelines*. Mahwah, NJ: Lawrence Erlbaum Associates.

Advocating a social justice agenda for children's universal right to basic education, Spring deals with the current debates around race, gender, class, and sexuality. In the process, he provides a powerful theoretical base for educational programs that are responsive to social, cultural, political, and ethical concerns.

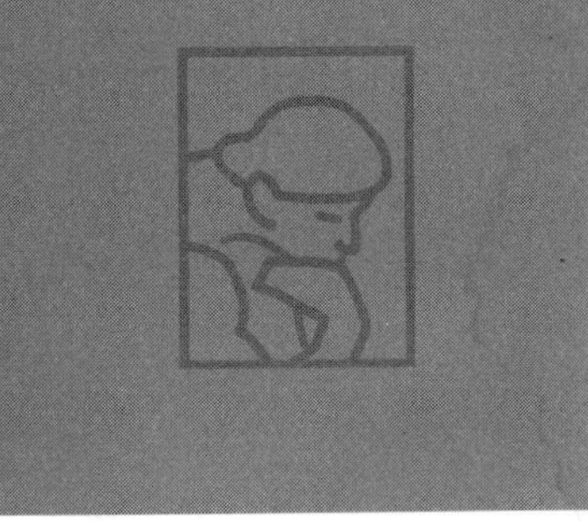

REFERENCES

Anyon, J. (1997). *Ghetto schooling: A political economy of urban educational reform*. New York: Teachers College Press.

Brause, R. S. (1992). *Enduring schools: Problems and possibilities.* London: RoutledgeFalmer.

Clark, C. M. (1995). *Thoughtful teaching*. New York: Teachers College Press.

Cowley, J. (1999). *Mrs. Wishy Washy*. Auckland, NZ: Philomel Books.

Harwayne, S. (2000). *Lifetime guarantees: Toward ambitious literacy teaching*. Portsmouth, NH: Heinemann.

Kozol, J. (2000). *Ordinary resurrections: Children in the years of hope.* New York: Crown.

Malloy, J. T. (1975). *Dress for success*. New York: P. H. Wyden-Warner.

Malloy, J. T. (1978). *The woman's dress for success*. New York: P. H. Wyden-Warner.

Paterson, K. (1977). *Bridge to Terabithia*. New York: Harper & Row.

Tyler, R. W. (1950). *Basic principles of curriculum development*. Chicago: University of Chicago Press.

Van Allsburg, C. (1981). *Jumanji*. Boston: Houghton Mifflin.

Van Allsburg, C. (1985). *Polar express*. Boston: Houghton Mifflin.

Williams, V. B. (1982). *A chair for my mother*. New York: Scholastic.

Index

D

E

F

G

H

I

J

K

L

M

N

O

P

Q

R

S

T

V

W